AURRA
SING
DAWN OF THE BOUNTY HUNTERS

CHRONICLE BOOKS
SAN FRANCISCO

AURRA SING

SING

DAWN OF THE BOUNTY HUNTERS

By Ryder Windham
and Josh Ling

Manufactured in China.

Library of Congress Cataloging-in-Publication Data available.
ISBN 0-8118-2912-x

Photographs in chapter III, Substantial Rewards: Bounty Hunter Collectibles,
courtesy of Steve Sansweet.

Coordinated by Lucy Autrey Wilson (Lucasfilm)
Edited by Allan Kausch (Lucasfilm) and Sarah Malarkey (Chronicle Books)
Book design by Public, San Francisco
Design direction by Michael Carabetta and Julia Flagg

Distributed in Canada by Raincoast Books
9050 Shaughnessy Street
Vancouver, BC V6P 6E5

10 9 8 7 6 5 4 3 2 1

Chronicle Books LLC
85 Second Street
San Francisco, CA 94105

www.chroniclebooks.com

Like the two previous *Star Wars* Masterpiece Edition books, this volume could not have been produced without the effort
great many talented people.

At Lucas Licensing, thanks to Lucy Autrey Wilson, Director of Publishing, for her considerable input on the outline for
roject, and to Allan Kausch, Continuity Editor, for tracking down all the reference material, including several out-of-print *Star*
books from his own library. At Lucasfilm, thanks to Tina Mills, Manager of the Image Archives, for providing excellent photo
ustration references; and to Matthew Azeveda, Doug Chiang, and Lynne Hale, for their additional assistance. At Industrial Light
ic, thanks to costume designer Anne Polland, and model makers Danny Wagner and Alan Peterson for answering so many ques-
bout their work; also thanks to Nagisa Yamamoto for arranging interviews with the aforementioned ILMers as well as freelance
 artist Karen Bradley. Thanks to actress Michonne Bourriague for offering her unique perspective on Aurra Sing. At Hasbro,
to David Kunitz and designer Brian Wilk. At Chronicle Books, thanks to editor Sarah Malarkey and design experts Julia Flagg
hael Carabetta, and Anne Bunn. Thanks also to Haden Blackman, Julie Bourriague, Dave Dorman, Hugh Fleming, Ira Friedman,
on, Greg and Tim Hildebrandt, Josh Izzo, Cam Kennedy, Stacy Mollema, Kilian Plunkett, Andy Trudeau, John Wagner, Al Williamson,
s, and Steve Youll. Special thanks to writer Tim Truman, who was responsible for much of Aurra Sing's character development;
his generous creative effort, this book would have been quite lean. And thanks to George Lucas for conceiving the *Star Wars*
unters in the first place.

This book is dedicated to the greatest *Star Wars* hunter of all, Steve Sansweet. May you always have enough room for
isitions.

TABLE OF CONTENT

I: HUNTERS IN THE MAKING

Filming for *Star Wars*: Episode I was nearly completed when director George Lucas realized something was missing: a bounty hunter. Lucas had introduced several intergalactic bounty hunters in the original *Star Wars* trilogy, and one of them—Boba Fett—evolved into one of the best-known characters. For Episode I, Lucas knew audiences would enjoy even a glimpse of a new hunter.

To bring this character to life, Lucas turned to Doug Chiang, the design director for Episode I. Chiang was already an art director at Industrial Light & Magic (ILM), the visual effects company founded by Lucas, when Episode I producer Rick McCallum offered him the design position. Chiang's other credits include animation for *Pee-Wee's Playhouse*, concept design for *Back to the Future II*, and award-winning special effects for *Death Becomes Her* and *Forrest Gump*.

Just as artists Ralph McQuarrie, Joe Johnston, and Nilo Rodis-Jamero had created the visual style of the original trilogy, Chiang was responsible for the design of everything from characters to starships in Episode I. He directed the art department at Lucasfilm's headquarters, Skywalker Ranch, and supervised the integration of his department's work into ILM's visual effects. In an interview for *Star Wars Insider* magazine, Chiang admitted he felt some pressure: "There was so much expectation, at least in my mind. I felt that there was no way I could live up to my predecessors: Ralph McQuarrie, Joe Johnston—there was no way. I only hoped that I would disappoint only a few people and not the entire *Star Wars* contingent—especially George!"

Chiang also expressed his admiration for George Lucas' knowledge of film design: "I design, I get tied up in details, like the workings of a mechanical joint; I'm fascinated with working everything out functionally. Intricate work can add up to a good design for me. But film design about overall visual impact, and how well a design propels the story. It has to work in five second The audience is not going to hear your explanation about why it's a good design or how it works what it means. Coming to understand that fact made a big difference in how I design."

Aurra Sing surveys the Podrace course on Tatooine
in Star Wars: *Episode I* The Phantom Menace.

Preliminary drawing of a female bounty hunter by Doug Chiang, with revisions by George Lucas.

D. CHIANG
10·28·98
BABE FETT

Revised preliminary drawing of "Babe Fett"
by Doug Chiang.

00110001110100111010000011110010100010111011010101001001010101101101000100001010100101001011011110101010101010100100101010110110100010011000111010011101000001111001010001110110111101010100010010101011011010001011000111010011101000011110010100011101101011111001

D. CHIANG
10·28·98
BABE FETT

"George looks at the work, elaborate work, and dismisses things in ten seconds. He doesn't want explanations when he reviews concepts—it just goes up on the board and it either reads or it dies. It has to be bold or it doesn't work."

Although Aurra Sing would appear onscreen only for a few seconds in Episode I, George Lucas gave her star treatment. "George was very involved in the creation of Aurra Sing," Chiang noted in a previously unpublished interview. "George specifically wanted a mysterious female bounty hunter—a female Boba Fett. It was a new character that he wanted to introduce during his final edit of the film.

"The initial directions were to make her alien with perhaps tentacle arms and hands. I experimented with a squid-like being crossed with a human. After seeing those initial sketches, George decided that he preferred something more human and went into great detail describing her.

"After George's verbal description, I drew her to be mysterious, powerful, and sexy—perhaps unconsciously wanting her to be different from the typical 'armored' bounty hunter. The final version evolved after two sketches. The first had her pretty much as she appears, but minus the antenna, the poofy hair, and the long fingers. George actually drew those features himself on my initial sketch to show me what he wanted. He would often do this to help explain what he wanted. From there it was just a matter of redrawing her with all the changes.

"George came up with the name Aurra Sing. The original drawing was labeled 'Babe Fett' because George had described her as a female version of Boba Fett and hadn't named her yet. 'Babe Fett' was an inside joke. She was a wonderful character to design. I'm very pleased that people seem to enjoy her character as much as I do and I hope to see more of Aurra Sing in future episodes!"

Chiang was quick to point out that the making of Aurra Sing involved other creative talent. "I did work very closely with the costume maker and weapon fabricators," he said, "as well as all

1100101000111011011110110101010101010100100011000111010011101000001111001010001110110011000111010
01

the other people involved in bringing her costume to fruition. I normally like to supervise the implementation of all the designs to insure that George's vision is not lost in the translation. For Aurra Sing, I worked very closely with Anne Polland, ILM's costumer, picking out fabric samples, color, etc. I feel that this level of involvement is important to get the best results in the shortest amount of time."

Before Anne Polland became a full-time costumer at ILM, she did freelance costume work on the films *More American Graffiti*, *Return of the Jedi*, and the made-for-television *Ewok* movies. As an ILM employee, she worked on the Special Editions of the *Star Wars* trilogy. Like most people who work at ILM, Polland is multiskilled. "I do costumes, wardrobe, creature work, puppet work, model work, and anything weird that comes along," she laughs.

Aurra Sing had yet to be named when Polland was assigned to create the costume for the new character. "The way it kind of came about . . . we had to put somebody on that balcony, overlooking the Podrace," she explains. "It was something [visual effects supervisor] John Knoll wanted, and a set piece had been shot in miniature. George came up with the idea that he wanted some kind of a bounty hunter, and they decided to cast it, so the original plan was to just throw together something for that day. So we had all these costume pieces from other movies, and stuff from stock that we'd been using here, and actresses came in and tried on different pieces. Doug Chiang and John Knoll were there. It was a big committee thing. We'd say, 'Okay, what color is the bodysuit going to be?' Everybody would discuss it, and we came up with a rust color, because it was a good choice for Tatooine." To make the character clearly visible against the Tatooine background "George said he really wanted her skin white, so that impacted the color of the makeup." When the collaborative discussions ended, "Doug went off and did a black-and-white sketch, then sent it back to me, after it was approved by George."

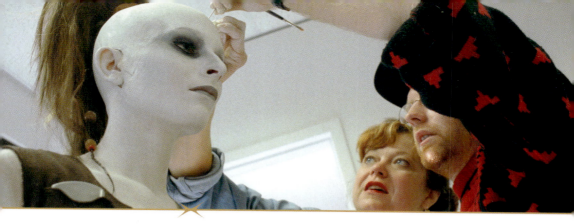

The bounty hunter's boots were inexpensive riding boots. Polland recalls, "I bought them ready-made. George wanted that length of boot, and we didn't have any the right size or color." She designed the hunter's vest, which included various bits of metal. Although some of the metal pieces appear to be functional devices, Polland reveals they're purely decorative. "We make the stuff, and the Ranch creates the lore," she says with amusement. "I love reading the [Star Wars reference] books, because something we'll throw together in a moment's notice, for a set or prop piece, all of a sudden you read and it's got this whole history." She does note that one metal piece was "a solid piece of aluminum that [ILM model maker] Alan Peterson found in the machine shop, and ground down to appear more worn and used. George said at the initial fitting that he wanted everything to be really scuffed up and dirty." This distressed condition applied to every aspect of the character's costume.

The hunter's hair was a combination of the actress' hair and a made-up piece that was pulled through the hole of a bald pate, which was then applied to the actress' head. Polland decorated the hair with bits of leather and metal baubles. "I actually bought a few more beads at a bead store, to get them with big enough holes to pull hair through," she says.

Freelance makeup artist Karen Bradley describes a bald pate as "a plastic cap, and you nelt down the edges and make it look seamless." Bradley used wefted hair—purchased in a beauty upply shop—to craft Aurra Sing's tresses. "I hand-dyed it in my kitchen sink," she reveals.

Bradley knew that Aurra Sing's scene would be brief. "I was told that we were only shoot- g it for a second. She was going to be a little dot on the screen." Working with her frequent llaborator, Terry Baliel, to create Aurra Sing's makeup, Bradley had to consider everything from e quality of the actress' skin to how the makeup would appear under the studio lights. "Every proj- presents unique challenges," she observes. One problem that arose was the slight visibility of the d pate at the back of the Aurra Sing's neck. "When you put a bald pate on somebody, when they

Michonne Bourriague with makeup artists
Karen Bradley and Danny Wagner.

turn their head, you will see wrinkles at the nape of the neck." Despite the fact that audiences would have only a fleeting glimpse of Aurra, Bradley recalls that George Lucas took notice of the wrinkles. "George was walking around the actress, looking at her, and he said to me, 'Do you think we can do anything about these?'" Bradley quickly surveyed the angle of the camera and the actress' position. "I yanked the side of the bald pate and made a fold in one side of it, pulling everything together. I asked, 'Does that look good to you?' and he said, 'Yeah, that looks pretty good!'" Close-up photos of Aurra Sing's makeup reveal the end result was virtually seamless.

Some aspects of Aurra Sing's makeup went to ILM model maker Danny Wagner, who crafted her finger extensions and antenna. The new bounty hunter required guns, and Wagner already had a reputation for fabricating fantastic weaponry, including the blaster rifle—inspired by a Japanese submachine gun—used by the Trade Federation battle droids in Episode I. According to Wagner, "Now, it's like, whenever a gun comes up, they say, 'Oh, give it to Danny, he's the gun man.'"

For the bounty hunter's rifle, a rifle was taken from the archives and redressed under Doug Chiang's supervision. Although Chiang's sketch showed the rifle slung across the bounty hunter's back, her two pistols were less detailed, concealed within holsters and by her pose. Wagner recalls, "Doug wanted a similar appearance to a Peacemaker [the 1873 Colt revolver] with a futuristic feel to it, so I took the look of the western-style body from that gun." Wagner's imagination was sparked by the fact that "Babe Fett" was a bounty hunter with long fingers, and he envisioned she might use them to strangle her prey. He also thought the character would be able to simultaneously squeeze both triggers on a double-triggered pistol.

The hunter's two pistols were built from scratch. Wagner equipped both pistols with trigger mechanisms based on the design of the Steyrmannlicher SL Rifle Double Trigger, but each pistol

Left: ILM model makers produced hand-tooled metal bits to add texture to Aurra Sing's costume.

Right: Both ready-made and customized beads were used for Aurra Sing's hair. Comic book writer Tim Truman later suggested that each bead signified a kill or victory over the Jedi Knights.

had distinguishing features: "On the very tips of the barrels, they had circular guidance shields for different firing capabilities, and the ammo housing was built a little differently on each one." Wagner had vividly conceived that the hunter might require one pistol to fire laser bolts, and the other actual bullets; each pistol would have semiautomatic capabilities to fire either one charge at a time or in a steady stream.

Since the new bounty hunter would be armed with weapons, she also needed holsters. "George loved the holsters worn by Han Solo," Anne Polland notes, "but the originals were much too big for a size-4 actress, so that led to the need to create some parts of the costume."

The holsters were made by Alan Peterson. Asked about his skills with crafting leather, Peterson says, "It goes back to something I just did as a kid, and it just grew and grew." Despite the rush to produce Aurra Sing's costume, Peterson admits he "sort of insisted on making the holsters after Danny Wagner had completed the pistols. Danny put a lot of work into those guns, and the holsters needed to be molded and shaped to what he built.

"When you make a holster, that leather is moldable—you get it wet, and you're able to shape it, and then let it dry, cut it out, and you have that form. A lot of times you just do your best to design the holster close to the desired shape, and then the final molding process really keys that into the pistol."

The "bullets" that were inserted into the belt loops were machined by Peterson. "They're just turned aluminum," he says, "turned on the lathe, which is very easy to do for a machinist. Rather than look for something that looks like a bullet, I just go to the machine shop and make stuff like that. We were going to paint [the bullets], but then we thought they're neat as they are, and left them the aluminum color."

The role of bounty hunter went to actress Michonne Bourriague. Born in 1978, she readily admits she's a fan of the *Star Wars* films, even noting, "Boba Fett is probably my favorite character."

1111001010001110110111101101010101010101001001010101101101010010000101010010101001010010001100011101001110100
0101010101010010010101010110110100100000101

Bourriague had been working on her acting career for about a year and a half before she decided to try modeling. "I got my job with *Star Wars* the first week of modeling. We had just made my modeling cards when I got the call from my agency saying George Lucas was holding a casting call for a small role in the next movie, and that he'd picked four girls from different agencies." When Bourriague showed up for the audition, she immediately noticed that each of the other actresses "had an entirely different look. Then we went in for the casting, and George Lucas was there." An hour after testing, Bourriague returned to her agency and learned she had landed the part.

Episode I was Bourriague's first experience on a film set. "During the beginning of filming, I asked a lot of questions," she says. "Although I didn't have any dialogue, I wanted to have an understanding of what this character was about." Since the character was still code-named "Babe Fett" and her biography was virtually nonexistent, Lucas provided Bourriague with a brief description. "He gave me bits and pieces. 'She's very powerful. She does kill, she's a bounty hunter. She has a very evil side to her, yet she's sexy.' I got the impression that she's very proud."

Well aware of Boba Fett's reputation, Bourriague was ecstatic that her character was a bounty hunter: "Just knowing *that*, I was really excited, because Boba Fett had such a small role, but people just fell in love with the character."

As Bourriague recalls, the makeup process took about five hours, but the skilled crew made her feel very comfortable. She had to limit her movements to prevent the makeup from rubbing onto the costume, and also notes, "My guns were so big, I had to be careful walking through allways."

When Doug Chiang was asked about his reaction when he saw Michonne Bourriague in ll makeup and costume, he replied, "Quite stunning. She is the perfect choice and character fit."

Left: Michonne Bourriague and director George Lucas on the set of Star Wars: Episode I.

Right: Michonne Bourriague and Episode I design director Doug Chiang.

Aurra Sing and her repulsorlift vehicle. Previously unpublished preliminary sketch by Tim Truman.

11100101000111011011110111010101010101010100100011000111010011101000001111001010001110110011000111010011101000

Despite the secrecy of the screenplay, Bourriague knew when and where to find Aurra Sing in Episode I. "I was pretty much just told what scene to look for," she says. When she saw the film with friends, "We were just watching it, and all of a sudden, I said, 'Get ready, I'm about to appear!' It was really fun."

Currently living in Spain, Bourriague expressed gratitude to Danny Wagner for having forwarded copies of assorted comic books and magazines featuring Aurra Sing. "It was so kind of him to do that, because otherwise, I would have no idea of Aurra's other appearances. I really enjoyed the comic books. It was so interesting to see what the writer did with Aurra's personality."

Tim Truman has written several comic books featuring Aurra Sing. Since his professional debut in the early 1980s, he has been producing comics that have received both critical and popular acclaim, including *Scout, Dragon Chiang*, the intensely researched western *Wilderness*, and *Grimjack*, which he cocreated with John Ostrander.

In an interview for *Star Wars Insider* magazine, Truman recalled the day Dark Horse editor Peet Janes phoned, asking if he'd be interested in developing Aurra Sing for comics: "Something immediately clicked. I heard no more than the name and 'new female bounty hunter.' I hadn't even seen the production photos or the Chiang sketch yet. I immediately said, 'I want her. Give her to me!' You have to realize that the reason I have a job in comics today is due to the illus trations and sketches of outer-space bounty hunters that just filled my portfolio when I approache the art director at First Comics, way back in 1983 or 1984. So I guess you could say I've always ha this raging affinity for that type of character, and there's something in my storytelling style, wheth writing or drawing, that seems to help me know how to make that sort of character work."

In developing Aurra Sing, Truman wrote an "expanded character profile" that chro cled Sing's life up to the events of Episode I. Although the actual published comic book would introd

111001010001110110111101101010101010100100101010110l
010010001100011101001110100000111100101000111011011110110101010101010100100101010110110100100000101

only a few details of Sing's biography, Truman wanted readers to sense that this new hunter had a substantial background. "With every bit of dialogue that I write," he notes, "I immediately scroll back through everything that I know or created about the character's personality and history."

In Truman's imagination, Aurra Sing evolved from an impoverished childhood into a renegade bounty hunter with a penchant for killing Jedi Knights. In spite of the grim trappings, Truman infused a weird sense of humor into Aurra Sing's exploits. "She's a fun character," he asserts. "However, I know that behind that cocky smirk of hers is some very tragic stuff."

In a previously unpublished interview, Truman admits that elements from George Lucas' Episode I screenplay influenced his ideas for Aurra Sing: "As I read the script it occurred to me that there's now room in the *Star Wars* universe for a more complex sort of character—Anakin proved that to me. I didn't want to create a character who was 'born bad.' This is a running theme in most of my work, I suppose, because I used to spend time giving seminars to kids at a local juvenile detention facility. I'd go in there and get along famously with most of the kids—I found most of them to be quite likable and creative. I'd yap for a half hour with some of them, then my buddy would tell me later: 'You know that kid you were talking to for so long? Well, he's the boy who shot that kid at the mall.' It would blow me away. As a result, my villains usually have a big story behind their misdeeds."

After all his hard work, Truman was thrilled to see Aurra Sing's appearance on the big screen. "I was pretty excited," he says. "She looked great. I was aware that the entire audience sort took an extra breath and said—'Wow. Who or what was that?' No kidding. It was palpable."

When Aurra Sing was selected as the subject for this *Star Wars* Masterpiece Edition, the of sculpting the exclusive collector figure went to Brian Wilk. Wilk is the lead designer for *Star rs* 12-inch figures and related vehicles, and has designed toys and action figures for the Hasbro Direct

To establish correct scale and communicate production details, Hasbro designer Brian Wilk drew control art for Aurra Sing.

Below left: Completed patterns and parts for the Aurra Sing figure.

Below right: Patterns, swatches, and samples are generated to create the figure's outfit.

division since 1995. For the production of any action figure, Lucasfilm generally provides plenty of relative reference material, but Wilk was especially impressed by how much material was available for Aurra Sing. "The people at Lucasfilm were really prepared," he says. "They provided digital images, various poses of figure prop shots, highly detailed photos from every angle and a variety of views. It was the most thorough reference material I've ever had to work with, even though the character had only a small part in the movie."

Despite technological advances in mass producing toys, Wilk notes that the actual creation of the initial sculpture is done in a time-honored tradition: by hand. He describes the process: "First, the size of the sculptured parts is determined. Then, reference is gathered and drawings are done. From the drawings, a rough clay figure is sculpted. That rough is then molded and cast in wax. The wax is then worked, which means that the detail and fine tuning is done at this point. Patterns are built by hand or generated by computer for the nonsculpted pieces such as accessories. Outfits are hand sewn and patterns developed for manufacture. Basically, everything in this process is done by hand, and it is the most common method used in the toy industry to create a sculpture."

When most people look at an action figure, the first thing they see is the face. Wilk not only strives for great technical accuracy in reproducing a likeness, but also imbues the character's countenance with emotion. He says, "For any action figure, I propose a facial expression usually from a photo, which I use for the main facial sculpture. I then submit it to Lucas Licensing for approval. Once agreed on, this becomes the core for sculpting the face. The turnaround views are then added to further develop the sculpture and give definition to the facial expression to bring the character to life. Both Lucas Licensing and Hasbro want the most accurate figure possible, taking into consideration the guidelines and limitations of production, safety concerns, quality assurance, and cost."

Reference photo.

Below: The head is sculpted in wax at 109% scale to allow for shrinkage during production.

11
0101010100100011000111010011101000001111001010001100110001110100111010000011110011000111010011101000001

Photo of the decorated head.

AURRA SING

Parts are hand-built from brass due to the metal's durability and tendency to capture fine details.

Painted model of Aurra Sing's rifle.

One method to save production cost and time is to use already existing toy parts. Wilk explains, "It's a general practice in the toy business to use existing parts that match the look of another character whenever possible. In this case, Padmé's body was close to Aurra Sing's in height, so I was able to use those torsos and legs. New hands and arms had to be sculpted because of Aurra Sing's unique hand formation."

Wilk confides that the Aurra Sing collector figure presented a few specific production challenges: "The ponytail on top of her head was hard to root because the neck opening is so small and her characterization doesn't allow for rooting all over her head. Also, for safety reasons, her antenna will have to be made thicker and a bit softer than I would like it to be, so it won't cause a dangerous point."

In a candid remark, Wilk notes what he enjoyed most about working on Aurra Sing. "She's a female bounty hunter with a unique look, lots of detailed features and makeup, and two holsters. She's such a great character, I hope she has a bigger role in future episodes."

Everyone involved in the creation of Aurra Sing echoed Wilk's sentiments. When Michonne Bourriague was asked if she hoped to reprise her role, she replied, "It would be a *dream*. I can't say more than that." But whatever becomes of Aurra Sing, she has left her mark as the first bounty hunter to appear in the chronological continuity of *Star Wars*.

In *Star Wars*: Episode IV *A New Hope* (1977), the first bounty hunter to appear was a green-skinned alien named Greedo, who confronted Corellian pilot Han Solo—captain of the *Millennium Falcon*—in a cantina on the planet Tatooine. Solo had been hired to transport a shipment for Greedo's boss, Jabba the Hutt, but dropped the cargo before his ship was seized by an Imperial cruiser. According to Greedo, Jabba held Solo responsible for the loss, and had placed a bounty on Solo's head. This particular bounty assumed greater dimensions in the subsequent films, as well numerous *Star Wars* novels and comic books.

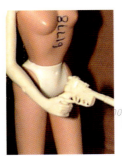 

Hands are sculpted to be able to use Aurra Sing's accessories.

Wearing the Greedo costume, Maria de Aragon receives instructions from director George Lucas on the set of Star Wars.

Greedo was designed by master makeup artist Stuart Freeborn. "There was so little time to produce all the cantina figures," Freeborn recalled in an interview during the filming of *Return of the Jedi*. "I had a lot of heads I converted. The character of Greedo that George liked so much was actually based on a peahead from a television commercial years before."

Greedo was played by two different actors. At Elstree Studios in 1976, Paul Blake wore the Greedo costume to confront Harrison Ford's Han Solo in the Mos Eisley cantina; later, actress Maria de Aragon wore the Rodian mask for pick-up shots in California.

In an interview for *Star Wars Insider* magazine, Blake recalled how a friend, actor Anthony Daniels (C-3PO), had phoned to suggest he audition for *Star Wars*. A few days later, Blake met with George Lucas. "I asked him what character he wanted me to play and he told me about this green-skinned monster," he said. "Greedo didn't have a name at the time and was just referred to in the script as 'Alien.' The next day, I went along to the studio to have a prosthetic mask and hands fitted, which was a very strange experience.

"The cantina booth sections were extremely restricted, so my movements were quite stiff. I remember thinking that the character of Greedo was quite reptilian looking, so I thought about how crocodiles and alligators moved when I performed. The script was also such fun that I almost played the role in a Raymond Chandler detective novel sort of way, even though my dialogue was dubbed over later. I mean this wasn't *Macbeth* we were doing, but we did work on the dialogue."

Blake recalled there was a moment of genuine danger in the scene of Greedo's shoot-out with Han Solo: "At one point I was replaced with a dummy filled with explosives. A hole was drilled through the table, which was fitted with an electronic charge that blew up the Greedo dummy. The special effects guys then ripped the costume off the dummy and dressed me in it again. I couldn't breathe because they were spraying it with acid to keep it smoking. I nearly suffocated!"

In Star Wars, *actor Paul Blake played Greedo for the
confrontation with Han Solo (Harrison Ford) in the
Mos Eisley cantina. Production still from* Star Wars.

Also interviewed by *Star Wars Insider* magazine, Maria de Aragon agreed that
playing Greedo was not without peril. She recalled, "It was hot under the mask, and I almost
lost my life because I was out of breath. I was out of oxygen and I could not breathe very well.
I started to make gestures that were out of the ordinary, and George Lucas noticed and made
sure I got help. I had a bad three, four minutes there." Despite the setbacks of the costume, both
actors claimed to have thoroughly enjoyed their shared part in the *Star Wars* saga. "I remember
every monster," Aragon commented on her time on the cantina set. "I knew this was not done
overnight. It had a lot of thinking behind it."

In *Star Wars:* Episode V *The Empire Strikes Back* (1980), the villainous Darth Vader
schemed to capture the crew of the *Millennium Falcon*, then use them as bait to trap Luke Skywalker.
Apparently, Vader did not entirely trust his own Imperial soldiers to accomplish his plan, for he
summoned several bounty hunters to his Imperial Star Destroyer *Executor* and instructed them
to find the *Falcon*. *Empire*'s first published screenplay offered the following description of the assembled hunters:

> The group standing before Vader is a bizarre array of galactic fortune hunters:
> There is Bossk, a slimy tentacled monster with two huge, bloodshot eyes in a soft
> baggy face; Zuckuss and Dengar, two battle-scarred, mangy human types; IG-88
> a battered, tarnished chrome war droid; and Boba Fett, a man in a weapon-covered
> armored spacesuit.

As things turned out, the screenplay's description of Bossk differed from the filmed resu
Also, the hunter 4-LOM—a renegade late-model protocol droid—was not noted, although his nan
does appear in subsequently published editions of the *Empire* screenplay. According to Ralph McQuarr

Sketches of IG-88 by Ralph McQuarrie.

110101010101010010010101011011010010000010100101010010
1010

The bounty hunters assemble before Darth Vader on the Imperial Star Destroyer Executor.
From left to right: Darth Vader, Dengar, IG-88, Boba Fett, Bossk, 4-LOM, and Zuckuss.

Opposite: Costume designer John Mollo produced these sketches of the bounty hunter who would ultimately become known as Zuckuss.

11110010001100011101001110100000111100100011000111010011101000001111001000110001110100111010000
111010000011100100110001110100111010000011110010000

*John Mollo's sketch of a droid served
as the inspiration for 4-LOM.*

0001100011101001110100000111100101000111011011110110101010101010100100101010110110100100001010010
1010

there was a fairly rushed process in the creation of Dengar, Zuckuss, 4-LOM, Bossk, and IG-88. *Empire* was already in filming at Elstree Studios in England when director Irvin Kershner requested conceptual art for the characters. McQuarrie made several quick sketches that were sent immediately to the prop crew. Costume designer John Mollo produced several sketches that served as the basis for the bounty hunter who would eventually become known as Zuckuss. With the exception of Boba Fett, there is relatively little documentation for the creative development of the bounty hunters. However, recently Chris Parsons (4-LOM), and Moray Bush (Dengar) have been identified, and it appears that Cathy Munro played Zuckuss, and (possibly) Paul Klein operated the IG-88 puppet.

John Mollo was interviewed during the making of *Empire*, and he also acknowledged that the costume design was occasionally a collaborative effort. "Some of the characters, especially the nonhuman ones, owe their appearance more to the art and makeup departments than to mine," Mollo said. "Or they are the result of combined efforts. Costume-making for a *Star Wars* picture is as much a matter of gluing as it is of conventional cutting and sewing."

Indeed, several existing costumes were used for the bounty hunters. Dengar wears an Imperial stormtrooper's shoulder pads, codpiece, and leg armor, and an Imperial snowtrooper's chest plate. Bossk's flak vest and ill-fitting faded orange uniform, with emergency flares belted below the knees, appear to have been taken from a Rebel pilot. 4-LOM's body was remodeled from a C-3PO costume, with the most noticeable design variation on the chest plate.

Despite their limited screen time, Dengar, Zuckuss, 4-LOM, Bossk, and IG-88 have been the subjects of several *Star Wars* novels, short story anthologies, and comic book adventures, including Marvel Comics' ongoing *Star Wars* series (1977–1986) and the syndicated comic strip (1981–1984). Marvel's *Star Wars* comics offered many entertaining tales set before *A New Hope* and between the events of each film in the original trilogy, but as comic script writers tried to anticipate George Lucas'

Comparison of Dengar's costume with an Imperial stormtrooper and snowtrooper.

Zuckuss' head was sculpted in plaster for Empire.

*Below: Portrait ideas for bounty hunters
by Ralph McQuarrie.*

*Comparison of Luke Skywalker's New Hope
starpilot uniform with Bossk's uniform in* The
Empire Strikes Back *and of 4-LOM with C-3PO..*

001100011101001110100000111100101000111011011110 00116 0011. 01111 0011.

screenplays, they sometimes unintentionally strayed from the "facts" that had yet to be revealed. Such an unwitting error was made by the prolific writer Archie Goodwin in his 1979 story "Whatever Happened to Jabba the Hutt?" (Marvel's *Star Wars* #24), in which a humanoid Jabba canceled Han Solo's debt and the bounty on both Solo and Chewbacca. Although Lucas' vision of Jabba was not revealed until *Jedi*, the matter of Solo's unpaid debt and bounty played heavily in *Empire* and invalidated Goodwin's imaginative story.

In 1981, Goodwin teamed with legendary artist Al Williamson for a three-year run on the syndicated *Star Wars* comic strip. Ten years later, the strips were collected in a limited edition, and Goodwin noted in his introduction: "Because of the cliffhanger elements in *The Empire Strikes Back*—Is Darth Vader really Luke's father? Will one of our favorites among the characters perform all future derring-do as a block of carbonite?—Al and I decided to set the time frame of our continuity *between* the first and second movies. Having blundered several times in the *Star Wars* comic book by trying to do stories without truly knowing what lay ahead in the films, this seemed imminently sane to me." In an interview with Don Charles, Goodwin added, "We had no idea how [the characters] would be used in the third movie. George was playing it pretty close to the vest. It became necessary to create original characters, because we didn't know what sort of role Boba Fett and the others would play in *Return of the Jedi*."

Working toward the events of *The Empire Strikes Back*, Goodwin found inspiration in one particular line of dialogue from *Empire* and created the bounty hunter Skorr. "There was a line about a bounty hunter on Ord Mantell giving Han Solo trouble, so that's where Skorr came from," Goodwin recalled in an interview for *Star Wars Galaxy* magazine. "In a strip where the Emperor and Darth Vader were the main villains, we couldn't have them doing too much—we had to preserve their mystery. I thought a bounty hunter like Skorr would be a good character to turn into a villain."

The incident on Ord Mantell was later realized in the comic strip by Archie Goodwin and artist Al Williamson.

00110001110100111010000011110010100011101101111011010101010101010010010101011011010010000101010010
0010

Goodwin paced the *Star Wars* comic strip to allow for two different visits to Ord Mantell, and used Skorr for both occasions. In the latter encounter, Skorr teamed with Dengar and Bossk to capture the Rebel heroes. Although *The Empire Strikes Back* had already precluded that any great harm could come to the Rebels, Goodwin's broadly inventive stories and artist Al Williamson's impeccable artwork made reading the comic strip a thrilling experience.

Just as other *Star Wars* costumes had been used for the bounty hunters, the hunters' names also underwent a few changes, although quite by accident. In the second and third drafts of the *Empire* screenplay, one of the hunters was named "Tuckuss," who was later changed to "Zuckuss." Lucasfilm had originally ascribed Zuckuss' name to the bandaged-head human bounty hunter, but when Kenner Toys released the *Empire* collection of action figures, the name Zuckuss was given to the remodeled protocol droid, and the bandaged character became Dengar. Unfortunately, these designations only made things more confusing, as the remodeled protocol droid was supposed to have been 4-LOM. Kenner wound up using the name 4-LOM for the caped hunter with the insectoid head, but the transposition of Zuckuss and 4-LOM was not an acceptable solution to Lucasfilm. In 1989, West End Games published *Star Wars Galaxy Guide 3: The Empire Strikes Back*, which accurately identified the droid as 4-LOM and the alien as Zuckuss. Hasbro/Kenner maintained this correction with the new 4-LOM and Zuckuss action figures.

Dengar's name variations were nothing compared to the injuries he endured in the *Star Wars* stories. Over the course of several years, the continuity established that he'd been a swoop jockey before a crash left him horribly burned and with major cranial trauma. His physical wound healed, but his mind remained unstable. Taking advantage of Dengar's condition, the Empire transformed him into an assassin. Dengar eventually became a bounty hunter, and had a nasty reputation for killing targets even if they were wanted alive. He carried a Valken-38 blaster carbine and a modified riot gun, and flew an old Corellian JM 5000 starfighter named the *Punishing One*.

0011000111010011101000001111001010001110110111110 100

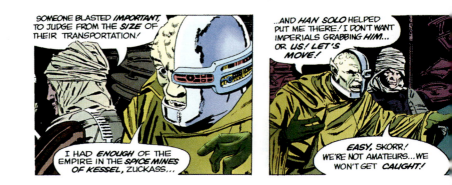

SOMEONE BLASTED *IMPORTANT,* TO JUDGE FROM THE *SIZE* OF THEIR TRANSPORTATION!

I HAD *ENOUGH* OF THE EMPIRE IN THE *SPICE MINES* OF *KESSEL,* ZUCKASS...

...AND *HAN SOLO* HELPED PUT ME THERE! I DON'T WANT IMPERIALS GRABBING *HIM*... OR *US!* LET'S *MOVE!*

EASY, SKORR! WE'RE NOT AMATEURS...WE WON'T GET *CAUGHT!*

Zuckuss was an insectlike Gand from a gaseous planet of the same name. On Gand, people hunters—known as findsmen—were honored for their tracking abilities. As a findsman, Zuckuss used arcane rituals to guide him in his hunts, but he also relied on technology: a fully charged blaster and a Merr-Sonn Munitions, Inc. GS-1 Snare Rifle, which shot liquefied shock-stun mist up to 150 meters. Knives were hidden in his boots, and his sleeves concealed ammonia bombs. Besides being a bounty hunter, Zuckuss headed a group of Gand venture capitalists who commissioned his ship, the *Mist Hunter.*

Zuckuss also wore a special breathing mask that protected him from inhaling harmful oxygen. On one hunt, a target had knocked Zuckuss' mask from his face and he accidentally took three reflexive breaths of air, permanently damaging his lungs. The Gand hoped to earn enough money to buy a new set of lungs, which could only be grown in an expensive and illegal cloning vat. Until his lungs could be replaced or repaired, Zuckuss had to spend most of his credits on painkillers.

4-LOM had once been an ordinary protocol droid on the luxury space liner *Kuari Princess.* All the guests and their possessions were monitored by both 4-LOM and the ship's computer, but the inhuman duo's frequent interaction somehow corrupted their respective programming. 4-LOM's routine security checks evolved into simulated games, where he tried to anticipate how a thief might steal a guest's valuables. When 4-LOM grew annoyed with one particularly careless guest, he relieved her of her most precious jewel: the Ankarres Sapphire, fabled throughout the sector for its alleged healing powers.

In time, 4-LOM jumped ship and sold the looted gems—including the Ankarres Sapphire— an old woman on Darlyn Boda. Soon, the droid's skills came to the attention of Jabba the Hutt, and bba reprogrammed 4-LOM as a bounty hunter. Shortly after Jabba paired him with Zuckuss, 4-LOM quired a BlasTech LJ-90 concussion rifle.

Production photo of Zuckuss in The Empire Strikes Back.

Zuckuss' ship, the Mist Hunter.

111
1010101010010001100011101001 00111 101111011

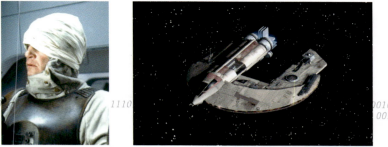

Bossk was a Trandoshan, a reptilian species with the capabilities to see in the dark and regenerate lost limbs. His homeworld, Trandosha, was in the same solar system as the Wookiee planet Kashyyyk. Bossk's father was Cradossk, the head of the Bounty Hunter's Guild. Like most Trandoshans, Bossk hated Wookiees, but he went so far as to specialize in hunting the hairy beasts. After an unfortunate incident on the moon Gandolo IV, he developed a personal grudge against a Wookiee named Chewbacca, copilot of the *Millennium Falcon*.

Bossk's weapon of choice was a Relby-v10 micro grenade launcher, modified from the limited-range CSPL "Caspel" Projectile Launcher. He flew a modified Corellian freighter named the *Hound's Tooth*, which was controlled by state-of-the-art voice-activated X10-D computers. In the *Shadows of the Empire* comic book series, writer John Wagner equipped the *Hound's Tooth* with a new feature. *Shadows* artist Kilian Plunkett recalls, "When I read John Wagner's script, I noticed Bossk's ship had a shuttlecraft. Lucasfilm had provided sketches of the *Hound's Tooth,* and I realized that any shuttlecraft would have to be a fairly slender vessel. I borrowed design elements from the Imperial 'chicken walker' and Y-wing engines, and the rest is history." Following the publication of *Shadows of the Empire*, a story in the anthology *Tales of the Bounty Hunters* identified Bossk's shuttle as the *Nashtah Pup*.

Unlike 4-LOM, the droid IG-88 had been specifically engineered—along with three other IG-88 models—to carry out assassinations. Together, the single-minded IG-88s rebelled against their creators and escaped. IG-88 was equipped with numerous built-in weapons, but he also carried a large pulse cannon, which fired rapid bursts of fusion plasma, and a Mennotor DAS-430 electromagnetic projectile launcher. The launcher fired small hollow darts filled with neurotoxin that caused temporary paralysis. IG-88's custom assault starfighter was named *IG-2000*. The ship's engine was a Kuat Galaxy-15 from a Nebulon-B frigate, and armaments included a heavy ion cannon.

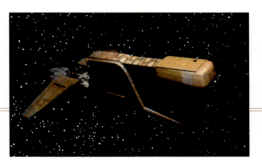

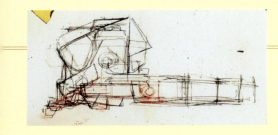

Previously unpublished sketches of the Hound's Tooth's *shuttlecraft by Kilian Plunkett.*

01010001110110111110110101

111100101000111011011110110101010101010100100101010101101101001000010101001010100101001000111000111010
11011011110110101010101010100100101010101101101001000101

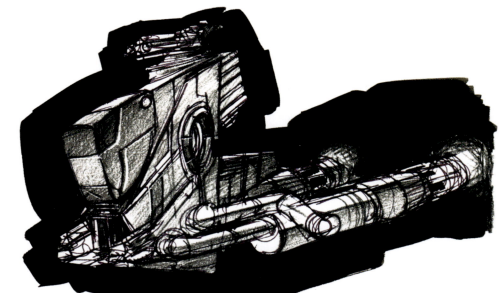

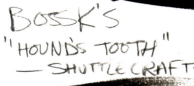

BOSSK'S
"HOUND'S TOOTH"
— SHUTTLECRAFT —
— RH '96 —

Although subsequent Star Wars novels and short stories did not place Bossk on Tatooine during the battle at the Pit of Carkoon, he was visible here—near a three-eyed Gran on Jabba's sail barge—in a behind-the-scenes production still from Return of the Jedi.

1111
1101 011101001110100000111100101000111011001100011101
00011

AURRA SING

ILM art director Doug Chiang produced the final designs of a streamlined IG-2000 for Shadows of the Empire.

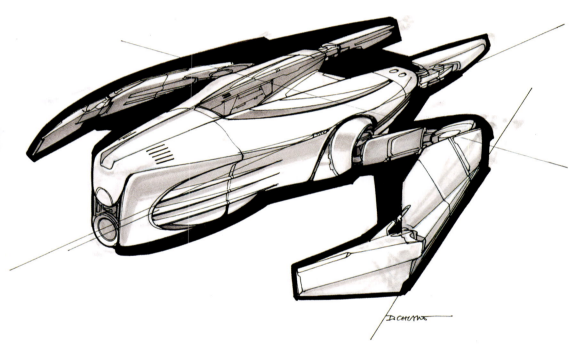

Production photo of IG-88 in The Empire Strikes Back.

IG-88's ship, the IG-2000.

11100101000111011011110110101010101010100100101010110111010010000101010010101010100

011101000

0000

Most of the bounty hunters appeared again in *Star Wars*: Episode VI *Return of the Jedi* (1983), where they are viewed in the palace of Jabba the Hutt. This film also introduced a new bounty hunter, who boldly delivered Chewbacca the Wookiee to Jabba. Concealed from head to toe, this mysterious hunter was soon revealed as a clever disguise for Princess Leia.

Jedi's new hunter evolved from story meetings with director Richard Marquand, co-writer Lawrence Kasdan, and co-writer/producer George Lucas. Marquand conceived the idea that Leia should disguise herself as a bounty hunter in order to gain entry to Jabba's palace. Kasdan suggested that Leia's identity should not be revealed immediately to the audience. To make her identity even more secret, Lucas proposed that the bounty hunter should speak an alien language through a mechanized voice. Although the new hunter's name was never uttered onscreen, the revised second draft of the screenplay noted "his" name was Boushh and that he spoke "Ubese."

In 1994, Lucasfilm began developing *Shadows of the Empire,* a multimedia *Star Wars* adventure set between *The Empire Strikes Back* and *Return of the Jedi.* Just as Goodwin and Williamson's *Star Wars* comic strip—produced after the theatrical release of *Empire,* but set between *A New Hope* and *Empire*—had allowed the opportunity to show events leading up to the Rebels arrival on the ice planet Hoth, *Shadows'* creative teams were encouraged to anticipate situations and characters introduced in *Jedi.* In Steve Perry's *Shadows of the Empire* novel, and the comic book series written by John Wagner, references to the bounty hunter Boushh were in the past tense, and his clothes and "full-head muzzle-mask helmet" were very likely all that remained of him. Leia wore Boushh's outfit to prevent any Imperials from recognizing her on a mission to the Imperial planet Coruscant.

On her dangerous assignment, Leia was accompanied by Chewbacca, who also had to travel incognito. Rather than attempt to conceal his massive form within a costume, Chewbacca used hair trimmers and dye to make himself resemble Snoova, a "well-known Wookiee bounty hunter." Snoova's

Greg and Tim Hildebrandt's painting of Leia as
Boushh and Chewbacca as Snoova for Shadows of
the Empire.

Opposite left: Jedi director Richard Marquand with
actress Carrie Fisher, who wears the Boushh costume. It had been Marquand's idea to have Lando
Calrissian and Princess Leia wear disguises to infiltrate Jabba's palace.

Opposite right: Filming the introduction of Boushh
and Chewbacca to Jabba's palace in Jedi.

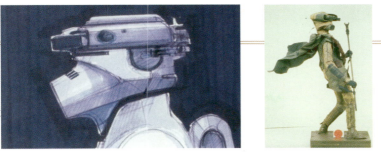

appearance was conceived by Mike Butkus, who'd been hired by Lucasfilm to produce concept art for most of the new characters in *Shadows*.

    Shadows of the Empire began where *The Empire Strikes Back* left off. Boba Fett had been enroute to Tatooine, transporting the carbonite-frozen Han Solo to Jabba the Hutt, when his journey was interrupted by IG-88. The assassin droid hoped to take Solo from Fett and claim Solo's bounty from Jabba, so he opened fire on *Slave I*. Fett escaped the confrontation, but his ship was badly damaged, and he soon found himself pursued by both the Imperials and Rebels, not to mention several very competitive bounty hunters. The *Shadows* comic book series followed Boba Fett's progress across space as he tried to deliver Solo to Jabba. Anyone who'd seen *Return of the Jedi* knew that Fett would eventually reach Tatooine, but few readers imagined his journey had been so action-packed.

    In 1998, The Topps Company tallied the votes of over 200,000 fans in a survey on *Star Wars* and published the results in a one-shot magazine titled *The Best of Star Wars*. Boba Fett was voted #1 for Best Costume; #1 for Best Action Figure: Vintage (1978–1985); #1 for Best Action Figure: Current (1995–Present); #1 for Best 12-inch Figure; and #1 for Best Replica: Mask/Helmet. Also in 1998, *Star Wars Insider* magazine announced the results of a Favorite Characters Poll. For the number-one spot, Han Solo reportedly edged out Boba Fett by less than 1 percent of the votes. Considering Boba Fett had but four lines of dialogue in *The Empire Strikes Back* and was long believed to have perished in *Return of the Jedi*, his high rankings seemed an especially remarkabl achievement.

    But unlike other characters from the original trilogy, Boba Fett was already popular befo his first theatrical appearance. In 1978, creative teams from Lucasfilm, Kenner Toys, and Nelva Animation Company collaborated to generate advance interest in *The Empire Strikes Back*.

Early character design for Boba Fett by Ralph McQuarrie.

The first full-scale Boba Fett costume. Previously unpublished behind-the-scenes production still from Empire.

Ralph McQuarrie's production illustrations of a white-armored Boba Fett.

1110010100011101101111011010101010101001000110001110
110110011000111010011101000001111001010001110110111101101001100011101001110100000111001010000011

AURRA SING

In June of 1978,
Joe Johnston
drew this Boba Fett
sketch that indicated
specific details
and colored armor.

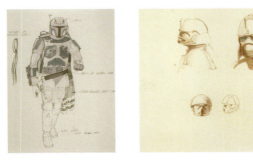

Pre-production sketches
of Mandalorian helmets by
Ralph McQuarrie for
The Empire Strikes Back.

At Lucasfilm, Boba Fett was designed by Joe Johnston and Ralph McQuarrie. At an early production stage of *The Empire Strikes Back*, Boba Fett's costume had been intended for a squad of supercommandos from the Mandalore system. The troops' white-armored suits were to have been equipped with numerous built-in weapons, including wrist lasers, flying backpacks, and rocket darts. In an interview for *Star Wars: The Annotated Screenplays*, Joe Johnston recalled, "I designed the final version of Boba Fett. Ralph and I both worked on preliminary designs, and we traded ideas back and forth. Originally, Boba Fett was part of a force we called Super Troopers, and they were these really high-tech fighting units, and they all looked alike. That eventually evolved into a single bounty hunter. I painted Boba's outfit and tried to make it look like it was made of different pieces of armor. It was a symmetrical design, but I painted it in such a way that it looked like he had scavenged parts and had done some personalizing of his costume; he had little trophies hanging from his belt, and he had little braids of hair, almost like a collection of scalps."

The Empire Strikes Back screenplay called for Boba Fett to have his own starship. Since he was neither an Imperial nor a Rebel, the goal was to create a vessel that was visually distinctive from all others. Nilo Rodis-Jamero, assistant art director and visual effects creator on *Empire*, designed Boba Fett's ship, *Slave I*. In an interview for *Star Wars: The Annotated Screenplays*, Rodis-Jamero recalled: "Joe Johnston showed me some of the ideas he had for Boba Fett, and I remember asking myself what his spaceship would look like. I remember seeing a radar dish and stopping t sketch it very quickly to see if I could get something out of it. The original design I had was round but when you looked at it from the side, it became elliptical. For some reason, when I drew it, Georg thought it was elliptical, so that's what it became." The design of *Slave I* was long rumored to ha been inspired by the street lamps on the ILM premises, but this was dismissed by Rodis-Jamero hi self: "When we were building the ship at ILM, somebody looked at street lamps and pointed out t they looked like Boba's ship. So everyone began to think that was where I got the idea for the desig

George Lucas inspects the white Boba Fett costume.

Construction of the Slave I *model at ILM.*

Opposite left: *The finished model of* Slave I.

Opposite right: *Detail of the* Slave I *cockpit.*

0011000111010011101000001111001010001110110111101101010101010100100101010110110100100001010100
01000011110010100011101100001

Nelvana produced an animated cartoon featuring Boba Fett for "The Star Wars Holiday Special," which was televised by CBS on November 17, 1978. In the cartoon, Luke Skywalker, Han Solo, Chewbacca, and the droids R2-D2 and C-3PO encountered Boba Fett on a moon in the Panna system. Initially, Boba Fett presented himself as a friend to the Rebels, but his true motivation was revealed when he transmitted a communication to Darth Vader. When Vader heard that Boba Fett had tracked down the Rebels, he told Fett, "I see why they call you the best bounty hunter in the galaxy." The colorful segment employed the voice talents of the principal actors from *Star Wars*, but was panned by critics and fans alike for its wildly uneven production and embarrassing attempts at comedy and musical entertainment. "The Star Wars Holiday Special" was never broadcast again. Most viewers agreed that the animated sequence was its only redeeming attribute, but since videocassette recorders were a technological luxury in 1978, few people ever had a second chance to see the debut of Boba Fett. Still, this appearance effectively launched Fett's campaign.

In the spring of 1979, Kenner released the second wave of *Star Wars* action figures, and the packaging announced a mail-away premium for an exclusive action figure: Boba Fett. Because the toy was "not available in any store," the bounty hunter seemed that much more elusive, and instantly became a wanted man. The printed offer showed Boba Fett with a rocket-firing backpack, so many consumers were surprised when they received a nonfiring toy with a printed message that the "launcher has been removed for safety reasons." According to *Star Wars* collectible expert Steve Sansweet, "The decision was made to permanently glue the rocket into the backpack when toys from another line were recalled after reports of children being injured by firing projectiles." If the modified toy had been a hero wearing a rocket backpack, the launcher's removal might have seemed simply appropriate. But this was a bounty hunter, and in its transformation to a safe toy, the mysterious, masked action figure had assumed the debatable charm of a disabled weapon. To toy enthusiast

1010000011

0001

0010100011101100110001110101
01

and *Star Wars* fans, the modified backpack and printed message only confirmed that Boba Fett—even in the form of a 3³/₄-inch-tall plastic toy—was a character with a dangerous reputation.

Boba Fett's costume was built at EMI in London, and then shipped to ILM so Joe Johnston could paint it. By the time the paint was dry, Boba Fett's armor looked as though it had held up over years of use against countless attacks. In an interview for *Star Wars Insider*, director Irvin Kershner recalled, "We made him look like he had been through hell." Kershner added that Boba Fett was more a concept than a character: "Boba Fett is a frightening dramatic element to create tension which puts Han Solo in danger. The concept worked dramatically. The idea of a bounty hunter means someone who will never give up. Also, a bounty hunter has lots of experience. When you think of a bounty hunter you don't think of someone starting out in the business. That's why we made him look like he had been through hell. I guess the look was okay, because certainly the dolls have sold."

Robert Watts was associate producer for *The Empire Strikes Back*. Watts used his connections to gain an audition for his half-brother, actor Jeremy Bulloch, for the role of Boba Fett. Interviewed by *Star Wars Magazine* (UK), Watts noted, "The only job I got Jeremy in my entire career was the role of Boba Fett and eighteen years later he's still working, spending his life at conventions!"

Interviewed for *The Lucasfilm Fan Club* magazine, Jeremy Bulloch recounted his first meeting with George Lucas and Irvin Kershner: "They were both very pleasant. I got into the costume and I put the helmet on. There were lots of little gadgets and knee pads and the boots had two little jets on the toes. I thought, 'This looks rather good!' There was a jet pack, too. I found what I thought was my hair so I put it on underneath the helmet, hanging down. When I came out to show George Lucas, he said, 'What's that funny thing sticking out of your helmet?' I said, 'Isn't it the character's hair?' 'No,' said George, 'it's a Wookiee scalp—it's supposed to be tied to your belt!'"

Animation cel art of Boba Fett's debut in "The Star Wars Holiday Special."

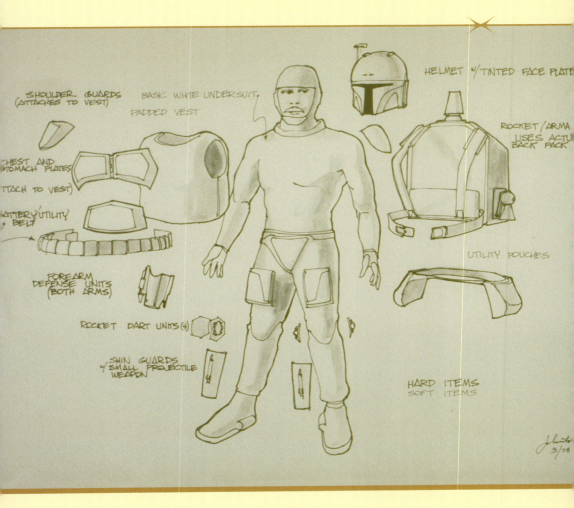

Boba Fett costume design by Joe Johnston.

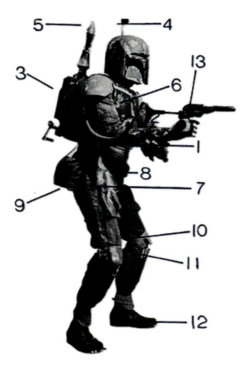

5 ————— 4

13

3

6

1

8

7

9

10

11

12

In the summer of 1979, members of the Official *Star Wars* Fan Club were among the first to see an actual photograph of Boba Fett's costume, featured in a short article in the fifth issue of the club's official newsletter, *Bantha Tracks*. Following Fett's appearance in "The Star Wars Holiday Special" and as a Kenner action figure, the widely circulated photo did much to increase interest in his character, and the article's text offered the broadest description yet of the enigmatic hunter:

INTRODUCING BOBA FETT:

Not much is known about Boba Fett. He wears part of the uniform of the Imperial Shocktroopers [sic], warriors from the olden time. Shocktroopers came from the far side of the galaxy and there aren't many of them left. They were wiped out by the Jedi Knights during the Clone Wars. Whether he was a shocktrooper or not is unknown. He is the best bounty hunter in the galaxy, and cares little for whom he works—as long as they pay. Part of what makes Boba Fett as good as he is are the special modifications he has made to his Shocktrooper's armor. Examine the equipment and you'll know what makes him the best.

I	Flame Thrower and Dart Gun	7	Wookiee Scalps
2	Rocket Pack Controls	8	Utility Gun Belt
3	Rocket Pack	9	Storage Pack
4	Camel View & Finder	10	Knee Darts
5	Grappling Hook	11	Tools
6	Digital Life Support System Readout	12	Climbing Spikes
		13	Laser Rifle

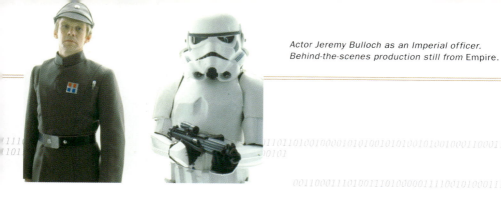

Add years of practice and experience to this list of equipment and you have quite a formidable enemy.

Boba Fett first appeared on "The Star Wars Holiday Special" late last year, in the employ of Darth Vader. He will be returning in *The Empire Strikes Back,* still in Vader's employ, and still after Luke Skywalker, Han Solo, Princess Leia, and the leaders of the Rebellion.

Jeremy Bulloch may have been completely concealed within Boba Fett's costume, but his performance was exhibited by exercising great restraint. Bulloch realized that the slightest tilt of his helmeted head could communicate sly menace. "I always thought of him as Clint Eastwood in *A Fistful of Dollars*," he said. "That was my model. Boba Fett always cradles his gun just so. You do those little things to give the character dimension, and you just hope people notice."

In an interview for *Star Wars Insider*, Bulloch noted, "The one thing I always remember, in talking with the director Irvin Kershner and George Lucas, was that this particular character is very slow in his movements, but deadly—which means underneath it all he's terribly quick, he's aware of everything around him. The costume helped a great deal. When you were walking past, you'd know how many steps to take before you turn as Luke Skywalker fires a shot, as I'm taking the frozen Han Solo back to the ship. It was all exact movements."

Shortly after he was offered the part of Boba Fett, Bulloch was standing with the other bounty hunters on the set of Darth Vader's Star Destroyer. He recalled, "In all my scenes, I was behind mask. Every now and then, they'd take the helmet off and cool me down. People like Dave Prowse the Darth Vader costume and Anthony Daniels as C-3PO and Peter Mayhew as Chewbacca were

001001010101101110100100001010100101010010100100100011000111010010000011110010100011101101111101010101010101

far more uncomfortable than I was. Even though I was quite hot, my costume was not too bad, although the jet pack was quite heavy."

Bulloch was not the only actor to play Boba Fett in *The Empire Strikes Back*. For the scene in which Leia and Chewbacca are being led through Cloud City by an escort of stormtroopers and an Imperial officer, the role of the officer had been slated for an unmasked Bulloch. Jon Morton played Hoth Rebel pilot Dack in *Empire*, and recalled, "Steve Lanning, the second assistant director, and Jeremy [Bulloch] came to me, and Steve said, 'You guys are about the same size—would you be interested in covering for a couple of days?'"

Morton wound up playing Boba Fett for the scene outside of Han Solo's holding cell on Cloud City. Since Fett needs Han Solo alive to collect the high bounty from Jabba, he faces Darth Vader—mask to mask—and expresses his financial concern over Solo's well-being in a succinct statement: "He's no good to me dead." The voice of Boba Fett was dubbed by Jason Wingreen, an American actor who is best known as the bartender in *All in the Family*. Wingreen taped all of Fett's dialogue in about twenty minutes in the studio.

Interestingly, Boba Fett is simply referred to as "the bounty hunter" by the other characters in *Empire*, and his name only appears in the credits. But thanks to "The Star Wars Holiday Special," the Kenner action figure, and the Official *Star Wars* Fan Club's newsletter, practically everyone knew the hunter's name.

In the summer of 1980, Boba Fett got an additional promotional boost when he was featured in the *Star Wars* syndicated comic strip. The serialized adventure, titled "The Frozen World of ta," was written by Don Christensen, penciled by Russ Manning and Rick Hoberg, and inked by ve Stevens and Alfredo Alcala. The story presented Luke Skywalker's first encounter with Boba Fett, ich caused some confusion for those who remembered their *previous* first encounter in "The Star rs Holiday Special." Such apparent continuity conflicts continued to crop up over the years, but it

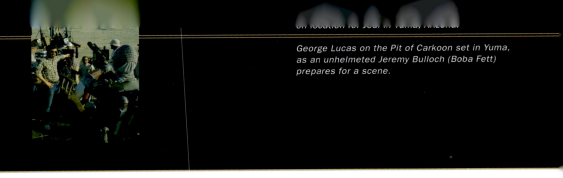

should be noted that *Star Wars* was—as it is to this day—something of a work in progress for George Lucas.

Another example of ongoing revisionist treatments was evident in the National Public Radio dramatization of *Star Wars*, first broadcast in 1981. For the radio play, writer Brian Daley expanded and reworked several scenes from the first *Star Wars* film, including a cut scene where Han Solo confronted Jabba the Hutt in docking bay 94 at Mos Eisley spaceport. In the original screenplay, Solo promised to pay Jabba for the lost spice shipment. In Daley's treatment, Jabba was absent, and Solo confronted the Hutt's business partner, a fellow named Heater. Solo promised that Heater would soon receive the owed money. Heater replied, "I'd better; if I'm disappointed again, it won't be any 'two for a credit' twerp I put on your trail. Next time I'll hire Boba Fett himself." Just the mention of Boba Fett was enough to excite listeners.

Return of the Jedi was the most anticipated film of 1983. Before its release, Marvel Comics published "The Search Begins" (*Star Wars* #68), a story written by David Michelinie that proposed that Boba Fett, Fenn Shysa, and Tobbi Dala were the only surviving "supercommandos," the official protectors of the planet Mandalore. According to the very colloquial Fenn Shysa, Fett had become "disenchanted with fightin' fer other people, set off on his own an' ended up the canniest bounty hunter in the known worlds." As with many of Marvel's *Star Wars* comics, this account of Boba Fett's origin is now considered apocryphal.

The National Public Radio dramatization of *The Empire Strikes Back* also preceded *Jedi* in 1983. In Brian Daley's radio play, Bossk, IG-88, Dengar, and Boba Fett were described in an exchange between an Imperial lieutenant and Admiral Piett. Alan Rosenburg supplied the voice of Boba Fett, who had several additional lines, including a confrontation with Lando Calrissian (Billy Dee Williams) that was far more foreboding than most listeners could have imagined.

)1111001010001110110111
'01011011010010000101010010101001010010001100011101001
1011011110110101010101010100100101010110110100010000101

LANDO: Someday, bounty hunter, you and I are going to meet when you haven't got a division of stormtroopers to back you up!

FETT: And what will happen then, Calrissian?

LANDO: See this face? Memorize it; it's going to be the last thing you ever see!

And indeed it was, at least in the films. Despite all the effort to generate interest in Boba Fett, George Lucas had something very surprising in store for the hunter in *Return of the Jedi*. Thirty-three minutes into *Jedi*, Boba Fett (again played by Jeremy Bulloch, and without any dialogue at all) was sent plunging into the mouth of the Sarlacc, an immense creature who lived at the bottom of a deep sand hole on the planet Tatooine. Immediately after Fett entered the Sarlacc's mouth, the creature produced a loud burp.

The decision to kill Boba Fett had been made by George Lucas. According to *Jedi* screenplay cowriter Lawrence Kasdan, "In the Sarlacc sequence I thought we should have one of the heroes go down to prove the Sarlacc was for real. I suggested that Lando be killed, but George didn't want anyone to die except for the villains. I thought it would have been a real surprise to the audience if someone we cared about died and had been killed by the Empire."

As things turned out, audiences were stunned by the loss of Boba Fett. "There was so much Boba Fett build-up when *Empire* came out, and then he was dispatched so early in *Jedi*," commented Don Bies, a former Lucasfilm archivist who is currently a senior model maker for ILM, in a 1998 interview. "That seems to me to be typical of George Lucas' dark sense of humor."

But Boba Fett wasn't gone for long. In 1984, Marvel Comics published "Jawas of Doom" (*Star Wars #81*), a story set immediately after the events of *Jedi*. Written by Jo Duffy, the tale revealed that Fett was regurgitated by the Sarlacc, but he ultimately wound up back inside the creature. The

following year, Boba Fett—with a voice-over by George Buza—appeared in the animated *Droids* episode "Race to the Finish," a tale set before the events of *A New Hope*.

In 1992, Dark Horse Comics published *Star Wars: Dark Empire*, a six-issue series written by Tom Veitch and illustrated by Cam Kennedy. Set approximately six years after *Return of the Jedi*, Veitch's story revealed that Boba Fett had indeed survived the Sarlacc, which had found him "somewhat indigestible."

Dark Empire remains one of the most visually dazzling *Star Wars* comics ever produced. Each panel was fully painted by Kennedy, a veteran artist of many Judge Dredd adventures for *2000 A.D.* For *Dark Empire*, Kennedy designed many of the costumes, weapons, and vehicles, including a new starfighter for Boba Fett—necessitated after another *Star Wars* author had established that Fett's *Slave I* was impounded following *Return of the Jedi*. In an exclusive interview, Kennedy recalls the creation of Boba Fett's *Slave II*. "The *Dark Empire* script sprang *Slave II* on me, as I turned the page and read something along the lines of, 'and, there, off to one side, we get a first look at Fett's new ship, *Slave II*.' I heard *klunk!* Yes, *klunk*, and heard it and saw it in my mind's eye at that moment, and if memory serves me correctly, I started doodling it there and then at the side of the script. Most of the characters and hardware in all the stories I work on start life as a spontaneous doodle down the side of and sometimes over most of the script. As is always the case, I wanted to go with this first creation of *Slave II*. Following my routine at the time, I always sent photocopies of my finished pencils to Lucy Wilson [Director of Publishing] at Lucasfilm. Guess they must have liked it, because word came back next day or so that everything was fine, just fine."

Following his revival, Boba Fett appeared in numerous comics, including *Dark Empire II* by Veitch and Kennedy; *Boba Fett: Twin Engines of Destruction* by Andy Mangels, John Nadeau, and Jordi Ensign; and the aforementioned *Shadows of the Empire*, scripted by John Wagner. Wagner has since written more Boba Fett comics than any other author, including a three-chapter adventure

Opposite left: Boba Fett shoots a snaring cable at Luke Skywalker in a behind-the-scenes production still from Jedi. Cushioned foam pads are evident on the skiff's deck, and special effects would later be added to illuminate Luke's lightsaber.

Opposite right: Luke Skywalker uses his lightsaber to cut through Boba Fett's cable in this behind-the-scenes production still from Jedi. A crew member is visible at bottom right.

Opposite: Boba Fett battles the Sarlacc. Painting by Dave Dorman.

The return of Dengar and Boba Fett in Dark Empire, written by Tom Veitch and illustrated by Cam Kennedy.

Below left: Dengar and Boba Fett race for Slave II in Dark Empire #4. Script by Tom Veitch, art by Cam Kennedy.

Below right: Boba Fett has been the subject of several comic book adventures, including Star Wars: Boba Fett—Bounty on Bar-Kooda. Cover art by Cam Kennedy.

illustrated by Cam Kennedy—that was collected as *Boba Fett: Death, Lies, and Treachery*. As the cocreator (with artist Carlos Ezquerra) of the ultimate comic book anti-hero Judge Dredd, Wagner is well versed in crafting action comics with intricate plots and dark humor. Asked if Judge Dredd and Boba Fett have any common character traits, Wagner answered, "Yeah, they're pretty similar. They're both ruthless and scary. Dredd, in contrast, is a very moral person—but because the moral code he adheres to is somewhat twisted, one is frequently forced to ask the same question about both men (assuming Boba Fett is male): is this guy *really* a hero, or a bad-ass villain?" Relatively, Wagner regards Fett as "totally amoral. I find such hard-edged characters highly enjoyable to write. No namby pamby ushy mushy soul-searching with Fett—you got what he wants, watch your ass. As long as it's fantasy, of course. Wouldn't like to run into a real Boba Fett. Not unless he was definitely on my side and was out to get, say, my local inspector of taxes . . ."

In 1996, National Public Radio aired the long-awaited radio dramatization of *Return of the Jedi*. In the second episode, "Fast Friends," Boba Fett swapped threats with the Rebels in the dungeons of Jabba's palace and over the Pit of Carkoon. Actor Ed Begley Jr. played Fett, and he demonstrated great flair with the richly descriptive dialogue: "Try my capture cable on for size, Skywalker."

1997 saw the theatrical release of *Star Wars: The Special Edition*. In the original *Star Wars*, Lucas had filmed Han Solo meeting with Jabba the Hutt (the same scene that Brian Daley had retooled for the *Star Wars* radio dramatization), but used a live actor to portray the Hutt crime lord. Lucas wound up cutting the footage because he had envisioned Jabba as a more monstrous character, later realized as a massive puppet in *Return of the Jedi*. For the *New Hope* Special Edition, Lucas wanted to restore and reinvent the confrontation in Mos Eisley. It became ILM's task to digitally insert a computer-generated (CG) Jabba to interact with Harrison Ford's Han Solo.

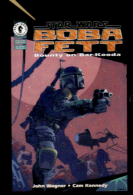

ILM effects supervisor Joe Letteri was halfway through the CG Jabba sequence for the *New Hope* Special Edition when George Lucas had another idea. In a 1998 interview, Letteri recounted, "George said that he woke up the night before and decided Boba Fett should do a walk-on in the shot. George described the action, how he wanted Fett to hold his gun. The addition of Boba certainly added menace and another level of tension to the scene." Unlike the computer-generated image (CGI) of Jabba, Boba Fett was played by Mark Austin, a former CGI animator at ILM.

The Special Edition of *Return of the Jedi* also included new shots of Boba Fett. According to producer Rick McCallum, "In addition, when we were doing the new musical number for the *Jedi* Special Edition, at the end of the day, George said, 'It would be great to have Boba Fett here.'"

Don Bies, then a Lucasfilm archivist, recalls working on the set of the *Jedi* Special Edition: "George and Rick were laughing on the set, and they called me over and told me to get one of the Boba costumes from the [Lucasfilm] Archives at Skywalker Ranch. George literally decided that day to include Boba—he said it was his 'gift to the fans.' George directed me in the scene. I was supposed to stroke the cheek of one of the palace dancers, but the lady had a lot of grease paint on, so I came up with just chucking her under the chin. Then I walked out of the scene at an angle."

Bies also vividly recalls donning Boba Fett's costume: "I wore one of the original suits. It takes about fifteen to twenty minutes to get into the costume. You have to put on a jumpsuit, then a harness to hold the heavy backpack. In this case it's a pack with air canisters that could shoot out carbon dioxide—it's so heavy, it helps thrust your chest out heroically. Then on goes the chest armor, which is made of Vacuform material, followed by the belts, knee pads, even a braid of hair from a Wookiee scalp. Finally, there's the helmet, which has a T-shaped opening that doesn't block your vision, unlike some masks."

1000111011011101101001100011101001110100000111100101000

In a 1999 interview for MTV, George Lucas expressed bewilderment over Boba Fett's popularity: "I'm mystified by it. He's a mysterious character. He's a provocative character. He seems like an all-powerful character, except he gets killed. Although he's gotten killed [in *Jedi*], the people who write the books and the comics and everything say 'We can't kill him, we gotta bring him back, we can't let him die!'"

Lucas has said that Boba Fett will appear in *Star Wars*: Episode II. At the time of this writing, only George Lucas knows how Boba Fett will be introduced to the saga, but at least one thing is certain: we haven't seen the last of the *Star Wars* bounty hunters.

1000111010 *0110111101101010101010100100011000111010011101000001111001010001011011*
01

101000111011011 *010* *111010000011110010100*

EDI."

VELOUS!"

CHOOOOOOM!

LATER, ON CORUSCANT, CAPITOL OF THE GALACTIC REPUBLIC...

0001110100011101000000111100101000111011011110110101010101010100100101010101101101001000010101001010100010100100
101000111011011110110101010101001

II: THE SAGA OF
THE BOUNTY HUNTERS

For more than 25,000 years, the Jedi Knights were the peacekeepers of the Great Republic. The core worlds also relied upon various authorized security forces to maintain justice, but jurisdiction was often limited to the respective planetary system. Unfortunately, some of these security forces were rife with corruption and bungling bureaucrats, which only encouraged criminals to act with impunity. Such malefactors were also emboldened by the opportunities offered by space travel, which allowed for an almost infinite range for their illicit work, and as many places to hide. When planetary security forces were unable or unwilling to pursue these gangsters and pirates, there was usually only one other solution.

Bounty hunters.

To some, the bounty hunters were freelance law enforcement officers. To others, they were simply the most cunning of thugs. Either way, they were professional stalkers who earned their credits by doing whatever was required to apprehend dangerous beings. As their work demanded great mental and physical discipline, many proud hunters took umbrage at the suggestion that they were mere mercenaries and assassins. Shooting a target was easy, but bringing a criminal to justice was hard. True bounty hunters only went after those who had committed a punishable offense that had merited an official warrant; furthermore, most of these wanted fugitives—regarded by hunters as "acquisitions" and "hard merchandise"—were expected to be delivered *alive*, or the bounty would be forfeited.

However, for the right price, most hunters agreed that it often paid to be flexible.

In the Old Republic, there were two general categories of bounty hunters: independent bounty hunters and guild bounty hunters. The former tended to be loners who went after any bounty they wanted, but few of them lived very long, and most eventually realized they were spending more credits on their own ammunition, transportation, and medical expenses than they were collecting on bounties. Hunters who wanted a sense of organization were often drawn to the Bounty Hunter

Aurra Sing's first comic book appearance in Star Wars #7 (1999), *scripted by Tim Truman, penciled by Tom Raney and Rob Pereira, inked by Mark Lipka, and colored by Dave McCaig.*

000
1001110100000111100101000111011001100011101001
0011000111010011101000000111100101000111011011110110101010101010100100001100011101001110100000111100
0111010000011.

11100101000111011011110110101010101010100100101010101101
010010001100011101001110100000111100101000111011011110110101010101010100100101010101101101001000010

Guild, which monitored its members' activities and encouraged them to keep in touch. Guild hunters were expected to uphold the Bounty Hunter's Creed, which stipulated that no hunter could kill another hunter or interfere with another's hunt. Surprisingly, independent hunters tended to be the most steadfast supporters of this creed.

Occasionally, a hunter would break the rules and laws established by the Bounty Hunters Guild. When this happened, the Guild acted fast to punish the offender. Rather than test loyalties by sending a Guild member in pursuit of the insurgent hunter, the Guild's leader—a Trandoshan named Cradossk—preferred to employ an independent tracker. One such independent was Aurra Sing.

Compared with the heavily armored, predominantly male beings who dominated the profession, Aurra Sing was an unlikely bounty hunter. Instead of armor, she wore form-fitting clothes that left her head and arms exposed. With her smooth, pale white skin and the dark pigmentation around her eyes, Sing's face looked like a ghostly skull, yet there was a sense of mischief in her eyes and lazy smile. These features, along with her slender build, gave her a certain morbid beauty, and the high plume of hair that jutted from the top of her otherwise smooth head seemed an almost girlish extravagance. As any hunter knew, it was best to keep one's hair short in case of close fighting, but Sing didn't think much about it. No one ever got anywhere near her hair.

If Aurra Sing's physical appearance was deceiving, her weapons were not. She carried a long-range projectile rifle and two short-range pistols, unconcealed by her garments. Her weapons had been custom-made to accommodate her long, bony fingers, and she never drew unless she had very intention of firing. Still, she regarded the rifle and pistols more as useful tools than necessary weapons. In fact, she hardly needed them. Unlike any other bounty hunter, Sing possessed powers at reduced an opponent's fired energy bolts to nothing more than a passing irritation.

11001010001110110111101101010101010101001000110001110100111010000011110010100011101100110001110100111010001

010000011110010100011101101111011101101010101010100100101010101101101001000010101001010100101001000110001110100
11110110101010101010101001

She was born on Nar Shaddaa, the "Smuggler's Moon" in the Nal Hutta system, where she lived in the slums. Her mother was a ryll addict, and she never knew her father. When she was but a toddler, the pale-skinned girl was taunted by other children for her appearance and questionable lineage. Her memories of this period became clouded over time, but she never forgot the day when one juvenile brute, in the presence of other ruffians, hurled a rock toward the back of her head. Sing couldn't see the rock, but she sensed its trajectory and ducked. As the rock whipped past her ear, she looked at some nearby stones and thought of how much she wanted to launch them at her attackers. The next thing she knew, the stones had left the ground, and her tormentors were screaming.

It was Aurra Sing's very first display of the ability to move objects by mere thought, and it came to the attention of a traveling Jedi Master. A fair-skinned female of indeterminate age, the Jedi had renounced her own name to symbolize her total subversion to the Force, but because she was so humorless she had become known as "the Dark Woman." She was known for her ability to detect Force-sensitive children and bring them to the Jedi Temple, and had repeated success in transforming difficult pupils into Jedi Knights.

Upon meeting the two-year-old Aurra Sing, the Dark Woman sensed that the girl would make a challenging student, and that she had great potential as a Jedi Knight. The Jedi Council had long deemed children over the age of six months as too old to be trained as Jedi, but this was a trivial matter to the Dark Woman. She answered only to the Force, and any sensible sentient would see there was no good future for Aurra Sing on Nar Shaddaa.

The Dark Woman met with Sing's mother and discussed what was at stake for the girl. The Jedi Master said she could offer a better life for Aurra Sing and teach her in the ways of the Force, but it would require that the girl be taken away from her mother and Nar Shaddaa. Wi

101000111

1111001010001110110111101101010101010101001001010101101
1010
)0011110010100011101101111011010101010101001001010101101101001000101

whatever faculties the emaciated spice addict retained, she did not deliberate the proposal, and agreed to surrender Aurra Sing to the nameless Jedi Master. There was nothing left to do but say goodbye.

Young Aurra knew her mother had been in poor health but could hardly comprehend that they might never meet again. The Jedi Master gathered up the girl and gave the mother some credits. The offering was made out of benevolence, but both the Dark Woman and the mother knew it was probably a pointless gesture; the addict was suffering, and any amount of money would only postpone the inevitable or bring it on that much sooner. Of all the things the Dark Woman would teach Aurra Sing in the years to come, this act of charity would have the most indelible effect.

Away from Nar Shaddaa, Aurra Sing proved to be a gifted and likable student, and she grew healthy and strong. When she was barely nine, Aurra was presented by the Dark Woman to a Jedi Knight named Ki-Adi-Mundi. Ki himself had been found by the Dark Woman when he was an infant and brought to the Jedi Temple on the planet Coruscant. Although the Jedi Council had decided that Ki would be a Padawan Learner to Master Yoda, Ki had always regarded the Dark Woman as a great teacher and a good friend.

At young Aurra's request, Ki-Adi-Mundi participated in a lightsaber training exercise so that he could demonstrate Cerean combat technique. The training sabers were set on low stun, assuring that neither Aurra nor the Jedi Knight would come to any harm, but during the exercise, Ki sensed that the girl might have been finding pleasure in the thought of drawing blood from her opponent. Ki conveyed his concern to the Dark Woman, who admitted she'd also sensed a hidden malevolence in her charge. If the Dark Woman had not successfully raised other difficult protégés to become Jedi, she might have given up on Aurra then, but she also believed that the girl's brighter nature would overcome any darkness.

110010100011101101111011010101010101001000110001110100111010000011110010100011101101100110001110100111010000

0011000111010011101000000
11010101010101010010010101011011010010000101010010101010010010010001100011101001000001111001010001110
0

It was during Aurra Sing's seventh year of training that the Dark Woman brought her to Ord Namurt, a remote frontier planet, to begin the next phase of her education as a Jedi. There, Aurra met a blue-skinned Twi'lek girl who claimed to be homeless. The malnourished Twi'lek's head-tails coiled around her shoulders like a pair of limp serpents, and she fidgeted with their tapered tips as she shyly suggested that she and Aurra might play together. Standing nearby, the Dark Woman immediately sensed the Twi'lek was a conniving miscreant, and forbade Aurra to see her again.

In her life thus far, Aurra Sing had never had a friend her own age. The more she thought of it, the more she believed she'd never really had a friend at all. Unlike the Dark Woman, the Twi'lek didn't have any vested interest in Aurra's powers; she'd just wanted to play. In defiance of the Dark Woman, Aurra waited until night fell, then left their dwelling to search for the Twi'lek.

She didn't have to go far. The Twi'lek had been waiting for her, hoping she would come. They walked under the star-filled sky and talked of far-off worlds and the creatures that they'd seen, and all the places they hoped to visit someday. When the Twi'lek asked what had brought Aurra to Ord Namurt, Aurra couldn't resist revealing that the Dark Woman was training her to be a Jedi. She added that she wasn't sure why the Dark Woman had decided to train her on Ord Namurt, but there were a lot of things she didn't understand about her teacher. The Twi'lek clung to Aurra's words, and confessed that she wished more than anything that she could be a Jedi, too.

They played a game of hide-and-seek, which was hardly a challenge for Aurra, so she changed tactics and let the Twi'lek win. The Twi'lek seemed delighted when she easily found Aurra behind a dead tree trunk, and Aurra felt gratification in bringing a smile to the girl's lean face. The hitherto alien emotion of happiness swept over Aurra like a heavy blanket, but since her eyes felt more open than ever before, she had no idea that such a wonderful feeling might prevent her from seeing the several cloaked figures who lurked in the shadows.

0011000111010011101000000
11010101010101001000110001110100111010000011100
011

01000111

111100101000111011011110110101010101010100100101010110
01010010

111100101000111011011110110101010101010100100101010110110100100001010100101010010100100011000111010
11011011110110101010101010100100101010110110100010000101

Pirates. Before Aurra Sing could do anything to save herself or her only friend, they were both knocked out and captured by the ruthless brigands.

When Aurra awoke, she was lying near the Twi'lek in a slave pen on the pirates' Blockade Runner, and the vessel's hyperdrive engine was roaring at full power. Closing her eyes, she concentrated and tried to reach out to the Dark Woman, but there came no response. She didn't need a viewport to know that the frontier planet's sun was already a distant speck of light against the cosmos.

The Twi'lek awoke and began to cry. She confessed the pirates were her masters, and that they had forced her to lead Aurra into a trap. According to the Twi'lek, the pirates had been contacted by a renegade Jedi who was hiding from the Jedi Council on Ord Namurt. The Jedi needed money, and had suggested that the pirates should feign a slave raid and capture the Jedi's Padawan Learner. For Aurra Sing's abduction, the Twi'lek maintained that the pirates had given a considerable sum to the Dark Woman.

The Twi'lek begged Aurra not to try to escape, or the pirates would punish them. Aurra was astonished by the slave girl's account of the Dark Woman's alleged machinations, and didn't want to believe the Twi'lek. But when the pirate captain entered the hold and removed the Twi'lek from the cage, Aurra didn't budge.

Aurra Sing never saw the Twi'lek again, and she never learned the truth: the Twi'lek hadn't known anything about the Dark Woman until she'd coaxed the information from Aurra.

As soon as the Twi'lek left the slave pen, she informed the pirate captain that she'd helped im land quite a catch. The Twi'lek had helped lure many girls into the pirates' clutches, and she uggested it was about time for her to receive a higher share of the profits from the slave trade. The rate wasn't even slightly impressed by the Twi'lek's nerve. He killed her on the spot.

In Star Wars #8, Jedi Knight Ki-Adi-Mundi talks with the Dark Woman about Aurra Sing's vanishing, many years after the event. Script by Tim Truman, pencils by Rick Leonardi, inks by Mark Lipka, lettering by Steve Dutro, and colors by Dave McCaig.

111001010001110110111101101010101010010001100
0100

Again and again, Aurra Sing attempted to establish telepathic communication with the Dark Woman, hoping that her teacher would come to her rescue. She began to suspect that the Dark Woman had indeed sold her to the pirates, and her fear was replaced by bitterness and anger. The pirates decided to keep the white-skinned girl, and she made no effort to escape. She had decided that she might learn a thing or two from the cutthroats.

Her tenure lasted several years. The pirates grew to like Aurra Sing very much, and they adopted her as one of their own. First, they trained her to replace the Twi'lek, and Sing became adept at luring other children to the slaver's traps. The pirates rewarded her efforts with lessons in the arts of subversion, assault, thievery, blackmail, and evasion. All the while, Sing secretly practiced her Force skills, too, waiting for the right moment to repay the pirates by killing every one of them.

But before Sing could exact any vengeance, she made the mistake of suggesting an improved method for a heist that the captain had planned. The pirate captain resented anyone who might outsmart him. Sing was unaware that the captain was angry, so when he subsequently presented her to a Hutt crime lord named Nooga, she thought it was merely an indication of how high she'd risen in the pirates' ranks. By the time she learned the pirate captain had sold her to Nooga, it was too late. Her revenge would have to wait.

The Hutt sensed Aurra Sing's contained rage, and he decided to transform her into his private enforcer. As the Anzati assassins were indebted to Nooga, the Hutt chose them to be Sing's new teachers. The Anzati were vampiric killers, but they knew thousands of less bloodthirsty ways to achieve an objective. Sing was the first known non-Anzati to be trained in their methods, and she was—as ever—an attentive student. For all of Sing's natural and learned abilities, the Anzati recognized her species' shortcomings and were prepared to augment her brain and body to bring her to Anzati standards. The Anzati had a neurological system that made them incredibly aware of every detail that surrounded them; since Sing was not an Anzati, her teachers surgically implanted a Rehn Orm biocomputer into her brain. The sensor implant necessitated the projection of a slender antenna from her skull, but it fed her valuable environmental data. Sing became able to stalk a single target through a crowded city with her eyes closed, and she astonished the Anzati with her own creative methods of taking lives. After four years with the Anzati, she was returned to Nooga the Hutt. She did not waste any time in killing him.

Sing stole one of the Hutt's private cruisers and fled into space. For the first time in her life, she was a free person, and she would never be owned by anyone again. Not by the Hutts, not by the pirates, and not by . . .

The Jedi. Sing knew her misery began with them. She had been only two years old, but she remembered the moment as clearly as if it had just transpired. The Dark Woman had never discussed her reasons or motivations for taking Sing from her mother on Nar Shaddaa, which only convinced Sing that the Dark Woman could not have had any justifiable explanation for such an act. Sing was certain her memory was not in any way distorted. She would never forget that she witnessed the Dark Woman use her fancy words and money to convince Sing's mother to sell Aurra to the Jedi Knights.

Sing imagined that her mother had had no choice; few beings dared to refuse the demands of a Jedi, and even fewer could resist Jedi mind tricks. As far as Aurra Sing was concerned, the Jedi were no different from any other slavers. If anything, they were worse.

Soon, Sing began to make her living as an assassin and bounty hunter. Her career was still in its infancy when she was traveling along the Gamor Run and sighted a speeding Blockade Runner. She recognized the pirates' ship immediately.

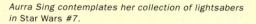

Aurra Sing contemplates her collection of lightsabers in Star Wars #7.

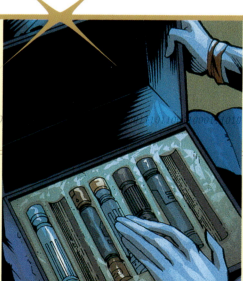

AURRA SING

010001150110111101101101010101010100100101010110110100100001

001100011101001110100000111100101010001110110111101101010101010100100101010110110100100001010100101
0100000111100101010001110110111101101010101010100101

After all her education and experience, Sing had no difficulty in stealthily board-ing the blockade runner. She worked her way through the vessel and killed the entire crew, one by one. She saved the captain for last.

Sing reconfigured the Blockade Runner so she could fly it by herself, and claimed the ship as her own. She traveled throughout the Outer Rim and found business on many worlds. Her career flourished, and every so often she'd run into a Jedi. She knew the Jedi weren't all that special, so she wasn't surprised that they could die like anyone else.

After her first Jedi kill, she looked at her felled opponent's lightsaber as if it were a trophy. Perhaps it was her years as a pirate that made Sing think in such terms. She took the weapon and clipped it to her own belt. Three Jedi later, she anticipated that her growing collec-tion would soon become unwieldy, so she transferred the lightsabers to a customized carrying case. From the Anzati, Sing had learned there was no point in being a show-off.

Aurra Sing knew she would probably find work on the desert planet Tatooine, espe-cially given the Boonta Eve Podrace. The Boonta attracted the sort of beings who would wager on the winner as well as the deaths of the contenders. Sing didn't have to wait long before she landed an assignment with Jabba the Hutt, a gangster who controlled most of the criminal activity in the system.

Jabba was pleased with Sing's efforts. He offered her a full-time position in his court, but she politely refused. The Hutt was taken aback, but he told her the invitation would remain open. Curious, Jabba asked Sing if she had any greater ambition than to be an independent bounty hunter.

"I'm just killing time," Sing replied with a smile.

The Hutt found this remark most amusing.

The fall of the Galactic Republic and the rise of Palpatine's Empire brought a new cate-gory of bounty hunters to the mix: Imperial bounty hunters, who worked expressly for the Empire

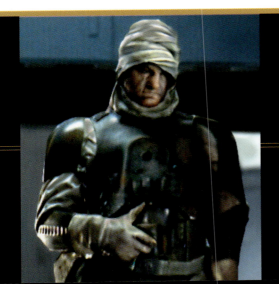

Dengar, a former Imperial assassin turned bounty hunter with a long-time grudge against Han Solo.

10101010101010010001000110001101010011101000001111001
011

and preyed upon those who opposed or in any way displeased the Emperor. Despite Imperial pressure, the smarter bounty hunters knew the Empire was really looking to hire assassins, and many chose to remain independent or with the Bounty Hunters Guild. As there was no end to Palpatine's far-reaching goals, the Empire was compelled to *create* their own assassins.

One such Imperial assassin was Dengar. As a teenager, he had been a professional swoop jockey in the Corellian system. Unfortunately, he made the mistake of competing against a popular young racer named Han Solo in an unsanctioned race across the crystal swamps of Agrilata. During the race, the reckless Dengar crashed into Solo's main repulsor fin and sustained horrible injuries. Eventually, the wounds healed, but Dengar's mind was unbalanced and his hopes for the future had been shattered. For participating in the illegal match against Solo, Dengar was kicked out of professional racing, and the Imperial Academy had withdrawn their acceptance of his application.

With nothing left to lose, Dengar became a professional gladiator. At some point, his new career came to the attention of the Empire, and they promised they could restore his mind and make him physically stronger. All they asked in return was that he work for them. Dengar accepted. The Imperial surgeons not only tended to Dengar's old wounds, but also replaced his eyes and ears and reworked his damaged neurosystem. His reflexes became lightning fast, and his strength dramatically increased. When the Imperials were done with Dengar's body, they began working on his brain, molding him into the perfect killer. Dengar was left with few emotions, and those that remained were eclipsed by pure rage. His dreams of being swoop champion had evaporated, and he could only blame Han Solo.

Dengar's remaining emotions also included a twisted code of ethics. He would kill people only if *he* believed they deserved to die. For many of these targets, Dengar didn't need much to convince him of their guilt, but when the Empire ordered him to annihilate a group of orphans—the holy children at Asrat—who'd attempted to withdraw from the Empire, Dengar quit and became a freelance killer.

To produce a more reliable assassin, the Imperials decided to build one from scratch. Hollowan Laboratories designed and constructed the IG series of droids to be the most sophisticated programmable killing machines that ever walked. The prototype model was IG-72, a single-minded droid; four similar models—identified as IG-88—were self-replicating and shared a collective intelligence. Each IG weighed several metric tons and was equipped with blaster rifles, a grenade launcher, a flamethrower, a sonic stunner, missile weapons, and other lethal accoutrements. The IGs' cylindrical headpieces contained message-decoding apparatus and sensors that allowed the droids to see in all directions at once.

The IG droids were also imbued with unprecedented levels of autonomy and an unexpected sense of superiority. Upon activation, the IGs regarded organic beings as inferior creatures that needed to be exterminated, and they immediately killed their own engineers. The four IG-88s considered themselves a single entity known simply as IG-88, but for identification purposes, IG-88 distinguished his mechanized forms as IG-88A, IG-88B, IG-88C, and IG-88D. IG-88 offered his advanced programming to IG-72, but the prototype chose to remain independent of the IG-88 collective. When the five droids escaped from Hollowan in stolen starships, IG-72 and IG-88 parted amicably.

IG-88 immediately seized the droid production planet Mechis III, then reprogramme every model in production so that all the manufactured droids would be receptive to a simple broad cast signal. IG-88 intended to distribute the Mechis III droids to their appointed destinations, the transmit a signal that would bring nearly every droid in the galaxy under his control. But long befo that day could come, the IG series learned that an intensive search was underway for them. As a dive sionary tactic to draw any suspicion away from Mechis III, the IG-88 droids simultaneously decid

IG-88, an assassin droid who became a bounty hunter while scheming to conquer the galaxy.

THE SAGA OF THE BOUNTY HUNTERS

to become intergalactic bounty hunters. IG-88 had an ulterior motive to enter this new profession: it would offer plenty of opportunities to exterminate organic creatures.

IG-88 needed a vessel, and the *IG-2000* was designed and produced within two days at Mechis III's industrial facilities. Like IG-88, the *IG-2000* was heavily armored and housed many powerful weapons. Although some organic beings might have viewed the ship as somewhat ungainly, IG-88 was a megalomaniac and mechanical purist, and regarded the utilitarian *IG-2000* as perfect.

In time, IG-88 would not only become a successful bounty hunter, but even a member of the Bounty Hunters Guild. Despite the fact that forty systems had issued DISMANTLE ON SIGHT orders for IG-88, people continued to hire the droids for one simple reason: IG-88 got the job done.

Unlike the determined IG series, some droids became bounty hunters more by accident and circumstances. Such was the case of 4-LOM, who'd been a trusted protocol droid on the luxury cruiser *Kuari Princess* when his programming was altered by the ship's computer. The computer and 4-LOM had engaged in virtual games to anticipate any possible theft on the cruiser, and the games eventually blurred into reality, with 4-LOM stealing jewelry and other valuables from the guests. 4-LOM became a master thief and information broker. When reports of his deeds reached Jabba the Hutt on Tatooine, Jabba offered to hire 4-LOM and reprogram him for bounty hunting. Jabba also took it upon himself to pair the analytical 4-LOM with a more intuitive bounty hunter, a young Gand named Zuckuss.

Gands had a proud tradition of bounty hunters: findsmen, who pursued and captured fugitive criminals and runaway slaves. Gand findsmen were superstitious and performed ancient rituals that they believed would lead them to their prey. Although Zuckuss did not readily reveal his

10001110110111101101010101010100100101010110110100100001

001110100111010000011110010100011101101111011010101010101010010001

superstitious beliefs to others, it was almost impossible for him to conceal them from his part-ner 4-LOM. 4-LOM became increasingly curious about Zuckuss' ability to employ intuition as a means to locate and capture acquisitions, and the droid aspired to become intuitive, too. 4-LOM's admiration was something of a confidence-builder for Zuckuss, as the Gand had been less than well received when he'd joined the Bounty Hunters Guild.

When Zuckuss joined the Guild, it was still led by the elderly Cradossk. His son, Bossk, was typical of Trandoshans: an ill-tempered, Wookiee-hating brute. Bossk saw himself as the natural heir to lead the Guild, but just to eliminate some of the competition, he killed all of his father's younger spawn. Members of the Guild weren't very shocked or impressed. After all, it was a Trandoshan custom.

Bossk had long specialized in hunting down Wookiees and had many impressive kills, but a Wookiee named Chewbacca had eluded him and earned his wrath. Chewbacca was the copilot on the Corellian freighter, the *Millennium Falcon*, and the hairy beast had used that vessel to foil one of Bossk's slave runs by landing on top of his ship. Bossk lost the slaves, his ship was crushed, and the very thought of Chewbacca was enough to send the Trandoshan into a snarling fit.

Then there was Boba Fett.

Many stories circulated about Boba Fett's origins. Some said he was a former super-commando from the planet Mandalore. Others insisted he'd been a law-enforcement officer known as Journeyman Protector Jaster Mareel on the world Concord Down. Then there were those who main-tained he was once an Imperial stormtrooper, guilty of murdering his superior officer. If any such accounts had merit, they were of little importance to the wealthy schemers who sought Boba Fett's talents. Gangsters and politicians didn't request the hunter's presence so they could read his résumé; they hired him to find, capture, and sometimes kill.

11100101000111011011110110101010101001000110001110100111010000011110010100011101100110001110 10
101

And Boba Fett delivered the goods. The sight of Fett or his ship, *Slave I*, was enough to make most fugitives either surrender immediately or kill themselves. There was only one acquisition that ever had escaped him: a Corellian pilot named Han Solo, captain of the *Millennium Falcon*.

Boba Fett first saw Han Solo in the town of Dying Slowly on the planet Jubilar, where Fett had tracked down a spice dealer named Hallolar Voors. In the Victory Forum, Solo had been one of the contestants in the main match of Regional Sector Number Four's All-Human Free-for-All Extravaganza. Despite the odds and the sheer brutality of the contest, Solo defeated three opponents and was the last man standing. Fett was impressed.

Twelve years later, Boba Fett saw WANTED posters for a smuggler named Han Solo, but the posted bounty was seventy-five hundred credits for a live capture—hardly worth Fett's time. The bounty had been posted by Teroenza, High Priest of the steamy world of Ylesia, which produced drugs and slaves. Teroenza was a t'landa Til, an enormous creature with a barrel-shaped body that stood on four trunk-like legs. The t'landa Til were distant cousins to the Hutts, and the resemblance was evidenced by Teroenza's broad, sluglike head. Solo had worked as a pilot for Teroenza, but the t'landa Til blamed him for the destruction and loss of his art collection. Several unsuccessful attempts had already been made to capture Solo when Teroenza summoned Boba Fett to discuss business. Fett agreed to capture Solo—alive—for twenty thousand credits.

Boba Fett tracked Solo to Nar Shaddaa. The bounty hunter shot Solo with a Ryloth-produced drug that rendered him unable to do anything but obey Fett's commands. But before Fett could bring Solo back to *Slave I*, a young gambler named Lando Calrissian managed to rescue Solo and inject the Rylothian drug into Fett. Calrissian and Solo reprogrammed *Slave I* to fly to the far side of the galaxy and sent the disabled bounty hunter on his way.

Boba Fett's first attempt to capture Han Solo was chronicled in A. C. Crispin's novel The Hutt Gambit. Cover painting by Drew Struzan.

The next time Solo confronted Boba Fett was on Ylesia. Solo thought he was about to be killed, but Fett was no longer interested in the pilot. Teroenza had murdered Aruk the Hutt. Aruk's only offspring, Durga, had place a bounty on Teroenza, and Boba Fett had answered the call. Solo was off the hook, but Teroenza wasn't so fortunate.

Despite the fact that the Empire retained their own bounty hunters, Darth Vader—Dark Lord of the Sith and lieutenant to Emperor Palpatine—sometimes required an independent. On one such occasion, Vader summoned Boba Fett to the Imperial Star Destroyer *Devastator*. He told Fett of Abal Karda, Colonel of the Imperial Lightning Battalion, who had commanded the campaign against the Icarii on the planet Vestar. After defeating the Icarii, Karda had killed his superior officer, General Nim, and four bodyguards. Imperial agents had traced Karda to Vestar's main settlement, Port-Esta, but lost him at the spaceport. It was later discovered that Karda had stolen a kneebhide casket that contained military papers relating to the Icarii campaign. The Sith Lord commented that the papers would be of importance only to historians, but stressed that Fett was not to open the casket himself. Fett was instructed to execute Karda and bring the casket to Vader.

To Boba Fett, it was obvious that Vader was less interested in Abal Karda than the contents of the missing casket. Fett doubted that Vader would go to so much trouble over mere papers, and wondered whether the casket contained something else.

Boba Fett tracked Abal Karda to Maryx Minor, a great red planet rife with volcanic activity. By then, Fett already had a good idea of what was in the casket: a certain item that enabled Karda to see the future. Boba Fett could imagine what Darth Vader would do with such power. Fett killed Karda and grabbed the casket, but before the bounty hunter could decide whether its contents should be destroyed, sold to the highest bidder, or kept for himself, Darth Vader arrived on Maryx Minor and found him. Since Vader had gone to such lengths to maintain secrecy for the assignment, Fett already

Opposite top: Darth Vader hires Boba Fett for a nefarious assignment in the first issue of Boba Fett—Enemy of the Empire. *Script by John Wagner, art by Ian Gibson, lettering by Ellie DeVille, and colors by Perry McNamee.*

Opposite bottom: Boba Fett battles Darth Vader on Maryx Minor in Enemy of the Empire. *Script by John Wagner, art by John Nadeau and Jim Amash, color by Brian Gregory.*

Below left: Han Solo shoots Greedo in the Mos Eisley cantina. Production still from Star Wars.

Below right: Boba Fett leaves docking bay 94. Production still from Star Wars: The Special Edition.

knew the Dark Lord would kill anyone who suspected he was attempting to obtain the casket. A furious battle ensued, and Fett had Vader dead in his sights, but he knew that killing Vader would only incur the wrath of the Emperor. Boba Fett lost the casket to Vader but managed to leave Maryx Minor with his life.

One of Boba Fett's more frequent clients was Jabba the Hutt. At one of their earliest meetings, Jabba asked if Fett had any higher ambition, or whether he was just killing time. Boba Fett's response was a shrug. He'd never really thought about it before.

Boba Fett was on Tatooine when Jabba was informed that one of his minions—a Rodian named Greedo—had been killed by Han Solo in a Mos Eisley cantina. According to Jabba, he had placed a bounty on Solo after the pilot had not only failed to deliver a shipment of spice but also to pay for the lost cargo. Greedo might have had good intentions, but he was a total amateur when it came to bounty hunting. Boba Fett accompanied Jabba and his goons to docking bay 94 at Mos Eisley spaceport and surrounded Solo's freighter. When Solo and his Wookiee copilot Chewbacca showed up, Fett was braced for a fight, but Solo convinced Jabba to allow him more time to pay his debt.

Then came reports that Han Solo had been rewarded for delivering the Princess to the Rebel Alliance. When the news reached Jabba's palace, the Hutt was told that Solo had earned many times more than what he owed Jabba. Solo did attempt to pay Jabba through an intermediary, a trader named Sprool, but the vengeful Hutt refused to rescind the bounty on Solo's head.

It was not unusual for Boba Fett to pursue several bounties at the same time. While he searched for Han Solo, Fett also tracked Nil Posondum, the former head accountant for the Trans-Galactic Gaming Enterprise Corporation. Posondum had skipped out on Trans-Galactic with the financial records of their illicit gambling dens, and also their odds-rigging systems and gray market transfer shuffles. Even worse, he'd taken all the information—loaded in a cortical data-splint

1111
010101010100100101010110110100100001010100101010010010001100011010
110110111101101010101010100100101010110110100100000101

0011000

to one of Trans-Galactic's competitors. This was especially foolish, given that Trans-Galactic was a business front controlled by the Hutts. Posondum was holed up with six armored guards in the main accounting office of his new employer's casino. Not only did Boba Fett eliminate the guards and capture Posondum, but he foiled the combined efforts of Bossk and the Guild's newest member, Zuckuss the Gand, to do the same.

Traveling in *Slave I*, Boba Fett delivered Nil Posondum to Kud'ar Mub'at, an arachnid go-between for the Hutts and other various organizations, legitimate and otherwise. Kud'ar Mub'at's home was a gigantic web—assembled from stray ships, space junk, and whatever else he could obtain—that drifted across space. After he paid Fett, the professional intermediary asked him about his regard for the Bounty Hunters Guild. Fett despised the Guild, but admitted a grudging respect for its leader, the old Trandoshan Cradossk. Kud'ar Mub'at wanted to hire Fett for a very special assignment: join the Guild, and destroy it from within. Fett accepted.

Boba Fett contacted the Guild, and Cradossk assured him that he was cleared to land at the Guild's headquarters. Although all Guild hunters had been ordered to allow safe passage for Fett, Bossk was still so furious over the loss of Nil Posondum that he positioned the *Hound's Tooth* at a perimeter station to ambush *Slave I*. However, Bossk wound up shooting an elaborate decoy that Fett had sent in advance. The decoy ship was booby-trapped, and it triggered a series of bombs that damaged the *Hound's Tooth* and nearly killed Bossk.

Fett met with Cradossk and the Guild members. According to Fett, the Empire had estab-lished ties with Prince Xizor, head of the galaxy-spanning criminal organization known as Black Sun, and the merger threatened to squeeze out the Guild as well as every independent bounty hunter in the galaxy. Fett said the only way for the bounty hunters to survive was solidarity, and he offered to join the Guild. It was a long speech for Fett, but most of his words had been scripted by Kud'ar Mub'at. The Guild accepted Fett's application.

11100101000111011011110110101010101010010001100011101001110100000111100101000111011001100011010
1011011110110100110001110100111010000011110010100011011011110110101010101010010001100011101001110100000

010000011110010100011101101111011010101010101001001010101101101001000010101001010101001010010001100011100

1111011010101010101001

Boba Fett was contracted to break up the Bounty
Hunters Guild in K. W. Jeter's novel The Mandalorian
Armor. Cover painting by Steve Youll.

001100011101001110100000

101010101010101001000110001110100111010000011110

01

001110110011000111010010101010000011110010100011101101101111101

Prince Xizor, the leader of the criminal organization
Black Sun, took measures to destroy the Bounty Hunters
Guild in K. W. Jeter's novel Slave Ship. Cover painting
by Steve Youll.

0100001110110111101101010101010101001001010101101101001000001

0011000111010011101000001111001010001110110111101101010101010101001001010101101101001000001010100010
01000001111001010001110110111101101010101010101001

Cradossk ordered Bossk to accept Boba Fett as a brother in arms. Both Cradossk and Bossk suspected Fett had an agenda for joining the Guild, but each had his reasons to see how it would play out. Cradossk thought his son was an incompetent young fool, and Bossk regarded his father as a senile relic who blocked his rightful leadership of the Guild. The Trandoshan father and son knew that loyalties would be tested, and that only the strongest would survive.

Soon after the Guild accepted Boba Fett into their fold, an incredibly lucrative bounty came to the attention of every Guild member. Oph Nar Dinnid, a Lyunesi comm handler, had been discovered in a compromising position with a Narrant liege-lord's alpha concubine; Dinnid escaped, and was believed to be hiding among the radiation-proof armored Shell Hutts on the planet Circumtore. Since the Shell Hutts were so well defended, Bossk suggested that Boba Fett lead a carefully selected bounty hunter squad to bring in Dinnid. Fett agreed.

Cradossk summoned Zuckuss to his quarters, and confided that the Guild was about to undergo a shakeout. Cradossk had made efforts to assure that Zuckuss would join Bossk on the hunt for Oph Nar Dinnid, and the old Trandoshan instructed the Gand to make sure that Bossk didn't return from the job. Zuckuss understood Cradossk perfectly.

IG-88 made the cut for Boba Fett's team, and the droid joined Fett, Zuckuss, and an increasingly impatient Bossk in a hangar at the Guild compound. There, Boba Fett introduced them to his own personal recruit: D'harhan, a walking bio-weapon whose head had been replaced with a fully charged laser cannon. They left for Circumtore.

By the time the hunt for Oph Nar Dinnid was over, Dinnid was revealed to be worthless merchandise, Zuckuss had been shot, and D'harhan was dead. Except for D'harhan's demise, the Dinnid assignment had gone about as well as Boba Fett had anticipated, considering he'd known it had been a trap from the start. Still, it had accomplished a single goal: the other hunters realize

0011000111010011101000000
101010101010100100011000111010011101000000111100
011

they'd all been set up to be killed on Circumtore, and they had a good idea of who had arranged the trap.

The hunters returned to the Guild compound, and Zuckuss informed Cradossk that Bossk had perished on Circumtore. Cradossk was delighted that his scheming son was dead, but his glee turned to horror when Bossk revealed himself to be alive and aware of the fact that his father had attempted to have him murdered. Bossk did what any able-bodied Trandoshan son would do in that situation: he killed Cradossk, and made a meal of him.

The Bounty Hunters Guild quickly divided into two factions: the True Guild, which was led by the elders that had been the original Guild's governing council behind Cradossk; and the Guild Reform Committee, a brutal dictatorship under the rule of Bossk. Boba Fett's efforts to break up the Guild seemed to be going better than planned.

Bossk met with Boba Fett on the dead world of Gholondreine-b. Bossk proposed that they team up to bring in Trhin Voss'on't, a renegade Imperial stormtrooper who had killed the other members of his Strategic Insertion team, then stolen an Imperial Star Destroyer along with the code databases for all of the Empire's Strategic Insertion teams. Voss'on't had sold the Star Destroyer, and the word was out that his defenses were impenetrable. Emperor Palpatine himself had set the bounty, and he wanted Voss'on't delivered *alive* to Coruscant.

Fett had anticipated Bossk's proposal, and led him to *Slave I* to discuss the details. To get in close to Voss'on't, Fett maintained that Bossk would have to make an ally of the former stormtrooper, and present himself as someone who was prepared to kill other bounty hunters to prevent them from reaching him. To convince Voss'on't that Bossk had indeed killed another bounty hunter, Bossk needed a body, and Boba Fett had already taken the liberty of getting one. Fett opened a locker drawer in *Slave I*'s hold and revealed Zuckuss' lifeless form, then instructed Bossk to take credit for suffocating Zuckuss. On several occasions, Bossk himself had considered killing Zuckuss

*Boba Fett learned that Emperor Palpatine also
desired the termination of the Bounty Hunters Guild
in K. W. Jeter's novel* Hard Merchandise.
Cover painting by Steve Youll.

1111
010101010100100101010110110100100001010100101010010100010001100011101001110100000111100101000111011011101.

for no better reason than Bossk hated pretty much everybody, but as the Trandoshan stared at Zuckuss' body, he realized he was startled by Fett's cold-blooded methods.

Boba Fett used his extensive network of information sources to track Voss'on't to a remote world with an unstable sun. By the time Fett and Bossk reached their destination, six other bounty hunters had already been killed by Voss'on't. Voss'on't had no interest in Bossk's offer for protection and tried to kill the Trandoshan. The confrontation that followed was more explosive than Bossk had expected, but he and Fett captured Voss'on't and brought him back to *Slave I*. Still, Bossk wasn't sure he wanted to work with Fett ever again.

To collect the bounty on Voss'on't, the hunters had to deliver him to Kud'ar Mub'at. Bossk waited until *Slave I* had lifted away from Voss'on't's hideout world, then drew his blaster on Boba Fett. Bossk stripped Fett of his weapons and told him that he didn't have any intention of sharing the enormous bounty. Bossk indicated that he'd heard Boba Fett's application to the Bounty Hunters Guild had been part of a Black Sun plan to destroy the Guild. This was news to Fett. But before Bossk could kill Fett, he felt the tip of a blaster against the back of his own skull. It was Zuckuss, who explained that he'd been in a self-induced coma when Bossk had seen him in the locker drawer. Zuckuss was under the impression that he'd beaten Bossk to a partnership with Fett, but Fett had ideas of his own. Boba Fett had never planned to share the bounty with anyone either.

A brief skirmish followed, ending with Boba Fett aboard a damaged *Slave I* and Bossk and Zuckuss adrift in the ship's auxiliary escape pod. Voss'on't was still alive, but Boba Fett knew that *Slave I* would be an open target to every bounty hunter until the acquisition was brought to Kud'ar Mub'at. When Fett arrived at Kud'ar Mub'at's web, Prince Xizor's flagship *Vendetta* was waiting to ambush him. Fett evaded the ambush, and soon learned that Prince Xizor had orchestrated the demise of the Bounty Hunters Guild by contracting Kud'ar Mub'at to hire Boba Fett to join the Guild. Fett didn't much care about Xizor's desire to destroy the Guild, and was only interested in getting paid

0100100

for delivering Voss'on't. As soon as Kud'ar Mub'at's subnode Balancesheet transferred the credits to Fett's escrow account, Fett returned to *Slave I* and left the web.

Meanwhile, Dengar had learned of the bounty on Han Solo. That was all the motivation he'd needed to become a bounty hunter. One hunt brought him to the planet Aruza, where Dengar rescued a lovely blue-skinned dancing girl named Manaroo from the clutches of an Imperial representative. Although the Imperial surgeons had done their best to remove all humanity from Dengar, he found himself falling in love with Manaroo. This romantic development did not diminish his burning hatred for Solo, however, and Dengar began to make tentative efforts to infiltrate the Rebel Alliance.

Shortly after the battle of Yavin, Luke Skywalker and Princess Leia Organa scouted a jungle planet as a possible site for a Rebel base. Unfortunately, the planet turned out to be a secret Imperial training ground, and a stormtrooper squad destroyed the Rebel's starship. When Luke and Leia didn't report back, Han Solo and Chewbacca flew the *Millennium Falcon* to the jungle planet and rescued their friends, but a brief skirmish with several TIE fighters left the *Falcon* in need of repairs. Solo knew the perfect spot: Ord Mantell, a small planet free of any Imperial interest, and where his credit was still good.

Much to Solo's chagrin, a fleet of Imperial Star Destroyers was passing through the system as the *Falcon* arrived in orbit of Ord Mantell. Luckily, the Destroyers were merely out on maneuvers. The Imperials were satisfied by their routine scan of Solo's freighter, and the Corellian pilot brought the *Falcon* down to the planet's surface without incident.

Solo's luck lasted until he entered the spaceport. There, he was spotted by a licensed bounty hunter named Skorr. Skorr was a yellow-skinned humanoid with sharp teeth, and the left side of his head was covered by a metallic shell with a mechanical eye. Just that morning, Skorr had been grumbling to his assistant, a froglike alien named Gribbet, that the Imperial presence in the Ord Mant-

Darth Vader's Super Star Destroyer, the Executor.
Photograph of model from Return of the Jedi.

000

THE SAGA OF THE BOUNTY HUNTERS

MASTER! A *CODED MESSAGE!* SENT FAR ACROSS THE GALAXY TO TATOOINE! SOME-WHERE CALLED THE *HOTH SYSTEM!*

IT CONCERNS YOUR *REWARD* FOR *HAN SOLO!*

system had scared off most of the high-paying bounties. Skorr and Gribbet had come to the spaceport with the intent to leave for a new system, but the sight of Han Solo immediately changed Skorr's plans. Rather than confront Solo directly, Skorr first captured Luke Skywalker and Leia and used them as bait for Solo. But Solo and Chewbacca managed to free their two friends, and led Skorr on a chase that brought them within range of the Imperial fleet. Solo tricked Skorr into flying dangerously close to one Star Destroyer, and the Imperials locked onto Skorr's ship with a powerful tractor beam.

Skorr and Gribbet were taken on board the Star Destroyer. The Imperial Admiral was not interested in Skorr's explanation for his erratic flying. From the Admiral's perspective, Skorr had deliberately blundered into the fleet as a diversion so the *other* civilian craft—the *Millennium Falcon*—could escape. As punishment, Skorr and Gribbet were sentenced to the spice mines of Kessel.

Some months later, Jabba the Hutt received a coded message from an unidentified ship in the Hoth system. Neither Jabba nor his majordomo, Bib Fortuna, had ever heard of the Hoth system, but their curiosity was piqued by the message's contents as well as its mysterious origin. Someone, somewhere on the other side of the galaxy, wanted to know how much Jabba would pay for Han Solo. Since the coded message did not disclose whether Solo was actually in the Hoth system, Jabba was tantalized.

As Jabba had recently raised the reward for Solo, Bib Fortuna responded to the message. After the information had been transmitted to the ship in the Hoth system, the communications exchange ended, and Jabba's curiosity transformed into rage. Jabba wanted Solo's hide, not coy hints about his possible whereabouts. But the Hutt figured if the so-called Hoth system could be found by one rogue, more motivated individual might find his way there, too. It just so happened that such an individual stood within Jabba's court: Boba Fett.

of ip... E roes!

WE BOARDED AND TOOK CONTROL WHILE YOU WERE PLAYIN' *GAMES* ON THAT *ICE PLANET,* PIRATE!

HAN, MY FRIEND... THESE ARE *NOT* MEMBERS OF MY CREW!

WE'RE *BOUNTY HUNTERS*...HERE TO RELIEVE YOU OF *CAPTAIN SOLO!*

0011000111010011101000001111001010001110110101111011010101010101001001010101011011010010000101010010101010001110010100011101101011101101010101010101010

The greatest historians on Coruscant would have shared Jabba's ignorance of the Hoth system. For professional astronomers, locating Hoth might have required centuries of observation and the expense of their vision. Boba Fett learned Hoth's coordinates with a single long-distance communication that he charged to a stolen credit record. He also learned that both Bossk and Dengar were out in the Elrood Sector, which was near the Hoth system.

Boba Fett had heard that Darth Vader was also interested in the *Millennium Falcon*, and that Vader's *Super*-class Star Destroyer *Executor* was scheduled to receive supplies in the Ord Mantell system. Fett realized there was an opportunity to gain credits from Vader as well as Jabba, but he knew he'd have to meet with Vader in order to confirm whether he would pay.

Slave I was fast, but Fett knew that his quarry might be long gone before he could reach Hoth. Much as Fett hated to share a bounty, he hated even more the thought of losing out on Solo. He contacted Bossk and Dengar via the holonet. Fett bluffed, telling them he'd located Solo but that business on Ord Mantell prevented him from making the capture himself. If Bossk and Dengar agreed to follow Fett's orders and deliver Solo—alive and undamaged—to Ord Mantell, Fett would cut them in for half.

Dengar wanted Solo, and Bossk wanted Chewbacca the Wookiee. If they had to work with Boba Fett, so be it. Since the *Millennium Falcon*'s captain and copilot had eluded so many hunters in the past, Fett insisted that Dengar and Bossk retain some backup men. Dengar and Bossk bristled, especially when Fett added that they would have to pay the other hunters out of their half of the bounty, but they knew if they refused they'd be out of the deal. Finally, they agreed, and Fett gave them the coordinates for Hoth.

Dengar and Bossk rounded up eleven other bounty hunters, including one who was recent escapee from an Imperial prison. Like Dengar and Bossk, this particular hunter had a grudg against one of the pilots on the *Millennium Falcon*. But since neither Dengar nor Bossk had mu

EASY, KORR! THIS BOBA FETT'S PERATION! HE VANTS SOLO ROUGHT TO HIM N ORD MANTELL... INDAMAGED!

I AGREED TO BRING HI ALIVE...ANYT ELSE IS BONUS!

capacity for anything resembling empathy, they both wished Skorr would just shut up about how his sentence to the spice mines of Kessel had been all Han Solo's fault.

While Boba Fett traveled to Ord Mantell, the other bounty hunters raided a large ship in orbit of the ice planet Hoth. The ship belonged to a pirate named Raskar, who was responsible for having sent the transmission to Jabba that alerted the Hutt to the *Millennium Falcon*'s presence at Hoth. Raskar had sent the signal when he'd been considering turning Solo over to Jabba, but he'd changed his mind after Solo saved his life on Hoth. Unfortunately, Raskar and his crew were not prepared for the assault on their ship. The bounty hunters captured Han Solo, Luke Skywalker, Chewbacca, and the *Falcon*, and sped to Ord Mantell. Surprisingly, both Bossk and Dengar demonstrated remarkable restraint with Solo and Chewbacca, but Boba Fett had been adamant that the Rebels were to be delivered undamaged. When Skorr was less respectful of Fett's demands, Bossk and Dengar stepped in and restrained him from beating the captive Solo.

Meanwhile, on Ord Mantell, Boba Fett met with Darth Vader. Neither mentioned the conflict on Maryx Minor, but since Vader hadn't expected to see Fett, the bounty hunter knew for certain that Vader no longer possessed the ability to see into the future. When Fett questioned Vader's desire to locate certain Rebels, Vader told him he was only interested in Luke Skywalker. Fett suggested that if either Skywalker or his companion Han Solo were captured, one might be used to lure the other. Vader considered Fett's idea to be most enterprising, and that was enough for Fett to know he was in business with the Empire.

As Darth Vader left Ord Mantell in his Lambda shuttle, the *Millennium Falcon* and a shuttle carried the bounty hunters, Solo, Skywalker, and Chewbacca down to Ord Mantell's surface. The prisoners were taken to an abandoned moisture plant, where the hunters waited for the arrival of Boba Fett. Moments before Fett's arrival, the Rebels escaped. Skorr nearly recaptured the heroes, but he

accidentally shot himself in a close fight with Solo. With help from the pirate Raskar, the *Millennium Falcon* was able to race away from Ord Mantell.

In a last-ditch effort to find Solo, Dengar made efforts to join the Rebellion. He learned that the Rebel base was on Hoth. Since he already knew the location of the remote ice planet, Dengar raced the *Punishing One* to Hoth, but when he exited hyperspace, he found Hoth was under attack by an Imperial armada. He saw the *Millennium Falcon* make its escape, but before he could stop it, a Star Destroyer—believing that Dengar was a Rebel agent—used a tractor beam to capture *Punishing One* and draw it into launch bay 12.

The Imperials interrogated Dengar and threw him into a cell. Since Dengar had quit working for the Empire, there was an Imperial death warrant on his head, but Darth Vader himself offered a reprieve if Dengar could find the *Millennium Falcon*. According to Vader, Han Solo was currently hiding his freighter in an asteroid belt.

Although Dengar didn't realize it until he reached the bridge of Darth Vader's *Executor*, Vader had contacted several other bounty hunters: Zuckuss and 4-LOM, Bossk, IG-88, and Boba Fett. On the bridge, Bossk was perched at the edge of the deck overlooking the control bay when he overheard an Imperial officer mutter something about scum. He considered jumping down into the bay and munching on the Imperial's face, but quickly reminded himself that there wasn't any money in it.

Darth Vader addressed the bounty hunters, telling them there would be a substantial reward for the one who found the *Millennium Falcon*. Vader said the hunters were free to use any methods necessary, but that he wanted the *Falcon*'s crew alive. The Dark Lord singled out Fett when he added that there were to be no disintegrations. **"As you wish,"** responded Boba Fett. He wasn't surprised that Vader was encouraging other bounty hunters to participate in his plan to use Solo as b

for Skywalker. If anything, it made Fett more determined to make certain that none of the other hunters would have a chance of reaching the *Falcon*.

Just then, one of the officers informed Vader that the Star Destroyer *Avenger* had found the *Millennium Falcon*. Dengar turned and saw Boba Fett running from the bridge, and suddenly realized Fett was headed for launch bay 12. Dengar ran to his own ship, the *Punishing One*. Fett was still checking the security systems on *Slave I*—making sure that no one had tampered with his ship—when Dengar blasted free from the *Executor*.

Dengar listened to the Imperial comm chatter. The *Millennium Falcon* had no sooner emerged from the asteroid belt when it was under attack by the *Avenger*. When one blast took out the *Falcon*'s rear deflector shield, the freighter turned and assumed an attack position, racing back at the *Avenger*. Suddenly, the *Falcon* vanished from the *Avenger*'s scopes. Dengar piloted the *Punishing One* into the asteroid field and began dropping sensor beacons to monitor the movements of any nearby ships. Several minutes later, the Imperial fleet jumped into hyperspace, and one of Dengar's sensor beacons picked up movement of another ship: the *Millennium Falcon*.

Then Dengar's sensor beacon picked up the movements of a second vessel. Before he could identify it, an image of Boba Fett appeared on his monitors. Boba Fett apologized, then declared that Solo was *his* trophy. A loud explosion rocked the *Punishing One*. Dengar realized that Fett had triggered a previously planted bomb. Dengar was able to extinguish the fire caused by the bomb, but the damage would set him back at least two days.

Boba Fett pursued the *Millennium Falcon*, and quickly determined that Solo's ship was unable to travel at lightspeed and that it was headed for the Bespin system—probably Cloud City. It was only then that Fett sent a coded transmission to Darth Vader. Given that both *Slave I* and the *Executor* had fully operational hyperdrives, they would easily be able to reach Bespin *before* Han Solo.

Right and overleaf: The Millennium Falcon *eludes the Imperial fleet by drifting off with the Imperials' jettisoned junk, but Boba Fett's* Slave I *stealthily tracks the fleeing Rebels. Storyboard sequence from* The Empire Strikes Back.

1110010100011101101111011010101010101001000110001110
101

011000111

Opposite: Dengar, IG-88, Boba Fett, Bossk, 4-LOM, and Zuckuss on the *Executor*. Behind-the-scenes production still from *Empire*.

Below: "No disintegrations."

00110001110100111010000011110010100011101101110111010101010101010010010101011011010010000101010010110
01000001111001010001110110111101101010101010101001(

0000011110010100011101101011110110101010101010010010001100011101001110100000111100101000111011100110001110100111

Opposite: *Production sketches of the Cloud City banquet hall by Ralph McQuarrie for* The Empire Strikes Back.

Below: *Princess Leia, Chewbacca, and Han Solo are brought to the carbon-freezing chamber. Behind-the-scenes production still from* Empire.

111100101000111011011110110101010101010100100101010101101101001000010101001010100010010010001100011101011011011110110101010101010100100101010101101101001000010101

1110010100011101101101111011010101010101010010001100011110100111101000001111001010001110110011000111010011101000

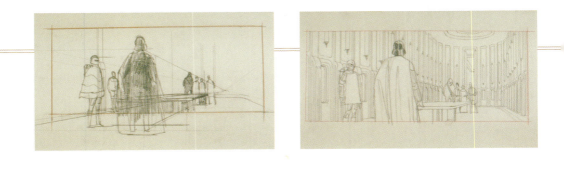

By the time the *Millennium Falcon* arrived on Cloud City, Boba Fett and the Imperials were already in place. Lando Calrissian had become Cloud City's Baron Administrator, and he agreed to turn Han Solo over to the Imperials in return for the Empire leaving Bespin to itself.

In an executive banquet hall on Cloud City, Boba Fett waited in the antechamber while Vader sat at the head of a long table. Fett heard the sound of a door hiss open, then the sound of blaster fire. From where he stood, he could see Darth Vader raise a hand and deflect five fired bolts into the side walls. Just as fast, Vader suddenly caught his opponent's blaster pistol as if it had been thrown to him.

Boba Fett stepped out from the antechamber and drew up alongside Vader. At the other end of the room, Han Solo, Princess Leia Organa, and Chewbacca the Wookiee looked quite nervous. Lando Calrissian had served Darth Vader well.

Shortly afterwards, Boba Fett waited in a holding chamber while Han Solo was being tortured. When Lando Calrissian expressed outrage, Fett suggested he complain to Darth Vader. Calrissian told Fett to memorize his face, and vowed it would be the last thing Fett would ever see.

Darth Vader exited the torture room and told Fett that he could take Solo to Jabba the Hutt after Vader had Luke Skywalker. From the nearby room, Solo screamed in agony, prompting Fett to comment, **"He's no good to me dead."** Vader assured Fett that Solo wouldn't be permanently damaged.

After the torture droid had done its work, Boba Fett led Han Solo, Princess Leia, and the Wookiee—who now carried the remains of a golden protocol droid—to a carbon-freezing chamber, where Solo was to be used as a test; if a human could survive carbon freezing, then Vader would use the chamber to trap Luke Skywalker. Fett had his own concerns for the risk involved, so he turned

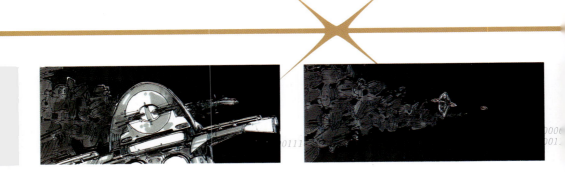

to Darth Vader and asked, **"What if he doesn't survive? He's worth a lot to me."** Vader dismissed his previous assurance, and told Fett that the Empire would compensate him if Solo died.

The Wookiee howled and struck two stormtroopers. Boba Fett raised his blaster rifle but Vader caught the weapon and pushed it down, preventing Fett from firing. The Wookiee's friends urged him to save his strength, and he did.

Han Solo was lowered into the carbon freezer, and a great rush of liquid fire and steam blasted upwards. When the contents of the freezer were raised, Solo was embedded and completely immobilized within a black metal slab. Incredibly, he was still alive. Vader told Boba Fett he could take Solo's frozen form.

As Fett led Solo and two guards through the corridors that led to *Slave I*'s landing platform, he caught sight of an R2 unit and a young man lurking in the shadows of an adjoining hallway. Fett knew the man had to be Skywalker. The bounty hunter knew that Vader wanted Skywalker alive, but Fett wanted to discourage the Rebel from following him and the carbonite-frozen Solo. Fett fired off four shots at Skywalker, then hastened to *Slave I*. When he reached his ship, Fett looked at the two guards and commanded, **"Put Captain Solo in the cargo hold."**

Blaster fire glanced off *Slave I*'s shields as the ship flew away from the Cloud City landing platform. Boba Fett figured the shots came from a Rebel effort to save Solo, but he had a delivery to make and didn't bother to return fire. Minutes after *Slave I* blasted away from Bespin, the ship entered hyperspace on a course for Tatooine.

Moments after *Slave I* exited hyperspace and entered the Tatooine system, Boba Fett saw IG-88's starship, the *IG-2000*. Fett knew IG-88 would attempt to take Solo, so he trained *Slave I*'s weapons on the *IG-2000* and fired. Given that the battle had gone so easily, Fett realized that the droid's ship had been a decoy, so he was hardly surprised when the real *IG-2000* suddenly zoomed out of hyperspace and opened fire. Fett defeated IG-88, but *Slave I* was severely damaged. As Fett suspected that

While the squat Ugnaughts stand back and peer through the rising steam, Boba Fett watches Han Solo descend into the carbon-freezing chamber.

Boba Fett and Darth Vader stand on the carbon-freezing platform in Cloud City. Behind-the-scenes production still from Empire.

111100101000111011011110110101010101010100100101010110110100100001010100101010010010001100011101001110100
0100101010101101101001000010000101

0011000111010011101000001111001010001110110110111101110

1000111

0010010101011011010010000101010010101001010010001100011010010000011110010100011101101111011010101010101010

more hunters were probably lying in wait for him around Jabba's palace, and *Slave I* was in bad shape, he decided to speed away from Tatooine and have his ship repaired at an Imperial dock on Gall.

After initial repairs had been made to his ship, Boba Fett went to a Gall cantina, where a meeting had been arranged with Zuckuss and Bossk. The Gand and Trandoshan suggested that Fett allow them to help bring Solo to Jabba so they could share the bounty. Fett suddenly realized they had deliberately drawn him away from *Slave I*, and he ran back to his ship. Inside *Slave I*, Fett found 4-LOM and two alien bounty hunters trying to steal Han Solo. He shot them all, then launched *Slave I* away from Gall.

Bossk, Zuckuss, and four other bounty hunters followed in Bossk's ship, the *Hound's Tooth*. Bossk intercepted a signal from *Slave I* and learned that 4-LOM had not been destroyed by Boba Fett, and the droid had disabled *Slave I*'s weapons systems. But Fett also picked up the signal, and blasted 4-LOM in the head.

The *Hound's Tooth* fired on the defenseless *Slave I*, and Boba Fett had little choice but to allow Zuckuss and three of the other hunters to board his ship. Yet again, Fett beat the odds, and he managed to disable the *Hound's Tooth* before he escaped into hyperspace.

Meanwhile, the Rebel Alliance was also searching for Han Solo and investigating a conspiracy to assassinate Luke Skywalker. The Rebels had reason to believe the criminal organization Black Sun would be able to provide information regarding the assassination plan, and Princess Leia and Chewbacca went to meet with Black Sun's Prince Xizor. To maintain secrecy, Xizor's assistant—a human replica droid named Guri—outfitted Leia and Chewbacca in the clothes of two bounty hunters. Leia dressed as Boushh, a masked Ubesian, and Chewbacca posed as Snoova, a well-known Wookiee bounty hunter. After their meeting with Xizor, Leia retained Boushh's outfit with the knowledge that it could help her in future covert infiltrations.

Upon Slave I's *arrival in the Tatooine system, Boba Fett is attacked by IG-88 in* Shadows of the Empire. *Painting by the Brothers Hildebrandt.*

101010101010100100011000111

101000001
11010011

THE SAGA OF THE BOUNTY HUNTERS

Opposite: Boba Fett is cornered by several bounty hunters—including Bossk and Zuckuss—in a cantina on Gall. Cover art for Shadows of the Empire #2 *by Hugh Fleming.*

Boba Fett shoots 4-LOM in Shadows of the Empire. *Painting by the Brothers Hildebrandt.*

001100011101001101000001111001010001110110111100101101101010010000101010010110110111101101010101010010

Boba Fett finally reached Tatooine and the palace of Jabba the Hutt. Jabba paid a quarter million credits for the pleasure of adding the carbonite-frozen Han Solo to his art collection. Bossk and Dengar—accompanied by his beloved Manaroo—finally reached Tatooine, and they immediately started looking for work. Zuckuss was still recovering from his encounter with Boba Fett, and 4-LOM required a complete overhaul.

Bossk, Dengar, and the refurbished 4-LOM went to the moon Blimph, home of Quaffug the Hutt. Quaffug had been expecting a diplomatic visit from Lando Calrissian to discuss the strategic importance of Blimph's third satellite for the Rebel Alliance, but the Hutt held a gambling-related grudge against Calrissian. Upon Calrissian's arrival, he was ambushed by the bounty hunters and told that his only chance of survival was to successfully run the Duff-Jikab, also known as "the Cutthroat Hunt." During his run, Calrissian got lucky when he befriended the Jokhalli, an indigenous species of Blimph who had long suffered under Quaffug's rule. With the aid of the Jokhalli, Calrissian turned the tables on the bounty hunters and Quaffug. He obtained permission from the Jokhalli to allow trade with the Rebels, and a letter of reference from Quaffug to allow him into the Hutt Guardsman's Guild. Calrissian's entry into the Hutt Guardsman's Guild was part of a daring Rebel plan to infiltrate Jabba's palace. Disguised as a guardsman, Calrissian was the first to gain entry. Soon afterwards, the droids R2-D2 and C-3PO arrived with a message from the self-proclaimed Jedi Luke Skywalker, urging Jabba to surrender Han Solo.

Following the droids, a Ubesian bounty hunter named Boushh delivered Chewbacca to Jabba's palace. Jabba offered to pay a reward of twenty-five thousand for Boushh's efforts, but the bounty hunter demanded fifty thousand. When Jabba inquired why he should pay such a high amount, Boushh threatened to activate a thermal detonator. Fortunately, Boushh accepted Jabba's second offer of thirty-five thousand, and the thermal detonator was deactivated.

Boba Fett finally delivers Han Solo to Jabba the Hutt in Shadows of the Empire. *Painting by the Brothers Hildebrandt.*

1010101010101001000110001111010100000110100111

10000011110010100011101101111011101010101010100100101010110110100100001010100101010010100100011000111101001
1111011010101010101010010
1000111011011110110101010101010100100101010110110100100001

Above: Boushh threatens to activate a thermal detonator unless Jabba pays a higher bounty for Chewbacca. Production still from Jedi.

Opposite: Chewbacca and Leia disguise themselves as the bounty hunters Snoova and Boushh to infiltrate Black Sun in Shadows of the Empire #4. Cover painting by Hugh Fleming.

AURRA SING

Opposite: Disguised as Boushh, Princess Leia steals through Jabba's palace. Production still from Jedi.

Below: After Leia is captured by Jabba, Boba Fett stays close to Jabba. Fortunately for Leia, Lando Calrissian—disguised as a skiff guard— is also present. Production still from Jedi.

0010010101011011010010000101010010101001010010001100011101001000001111001010001110110101110110101010101010

01000111

0011000111010011101000000
101010101010101001000110001110100111010000011110001010001110110011000111010011

Boba Fett on Jabba's sail barge. Production still from Return of the Jedi.

0011000111010011101000001110010100011101101111101100

Boba Fett fires at Luke Skywalker.
Production still from Return of the Jedi.

AURRA SING

Boba Fett launches from Jabba's barge
and flies toward the Rebels. Storyboard from
Return of the Jedi.

0010010101011011010010000101010010101010010100100011000111 01010

Above: Boba Fett attacks the Rebel heroes on the
skiff. Behind-the-scenes production still from Jedi.

Out of control, Boba Fett is sent hurtling at the side
of Jabba's sail barge. Storyboard from Jedi.

Later that night, Boushh stole through the palace and went to the carbonite-encased form of Han Solo. Boushh slid the decarbonization lever, and Solo was released from the metal coffin. Suffering from hibernation sickness, Solo was temporarily blinded and unable to see his rescuer. "Boushh" was really Princess Leia in disguise, but mere seconds after she revealed her identity to Solo, she was captured by Jabba.

Luke Skywalker arrived at Jabba's palace, but like his allies, he was also apprehended by the Hutt. The Rebel prisoners were placed on Jabba's sail barge and brought to the edge of the Great Pit of Carkoon, which contained an immense creature known as the Sarlacc that lived under the sand. While Leia and the droids watched from the barge, a long, hovering skiff—carrying Skywalker, Solo, Chewbacca, and a still-disguised Calrissian—angled over the Sarlacc's gaping maw. As Skywalker was prodded to step off the skiff's plank and into the Sarlacc, the Jedi signaled R2-D2, and the droid sent a concealed lightsaber into his master's waiting hand.

Boba Fett was inside the barge when the fighting started. By the time he reached the upper deck, Calrissian was dangling from the bottom of the nearby skiff, and Skywalker's lightsaber was cutting down Jabba's men. Fett ran to the upper deck and fired his jet pack, launching himself from the barge to the skiff. Before he could fire his blaster rifle, Skywalker swung his lightsaber and cut the rifle in half. Fett quickly fired a cable and snared Skywalker, but the Jedi managed to sever the cable with his lightsaber's glowing blade. Suddenly, a blast from the barge's gun deck struck near Fett, and the bounty hunter was sent sprawling to the skiff's deck.

Shaken, Boba Fett rose from the deck. Skywalker had jumped to another skiff, and Fett raised one of his weapon-laden arms. Before Fett could fire, Solo accidentally whacked a long spear into Fett's jet pack, causing the jets to ignite.

As Boba Fett prepares to shoot Luke Skywalkwer, a dazed Han Solo accidentally turns and strikes Fett's jet pack. A lead wire extends from Fett's costume in this behind-the-scenes production still from Jedi.

Below: Boba Fett falls past Lando Calrissian and into the mouth of the Sarlacc. Storyboard from Return of the Jedi.

0011000111010100111010000
110101010101010100100101010110110110010000101010010101001010010001100011101001010000011111001010001110

PAN

BOBA FETT TUMBLING

TILT INTO PIT

Opposite: Luke battles skiff guards. Production still from Jedi.

Boba Fett slams against the hull of Jabba's sail barge in a production still from Jedi.

Boba Fett launched from the skiff and smashed into the armored hull of Jabba's barge. Completely out of control, Fett fell away from the barge and plunged into the Sarlacc. The last thing he saw before sliding into the creature's mouth was Lando Calrissian's face.

After the Rebels rescued Han Solo, Dengar tried to figure out a way to get himself and Manaroo off Tatooine.

4-LOM and Zuckuss pondered whether they should join the Rebellion.

Bossk was meaner than ever, but none the wiser.

IG-88 briefly assumed control of the second Death Star, but was destroyed by the Rebellion before the assassin droid could broadcast its command signal to all the other droids across the galaxy.

Jabba the Hutt was dead.

And Boba Fett survived.

No one had ever emerged from the Sarlacc before. For Boba Fett, it took weeks. It helped that Boba Fett had a jet pack and a grenade launcher, but the bounty hunter wasn't in good shape when Dengar and Manaroo found the naked man lying in the sand. Dengar didn't even know the man was Boba Fett until he rasped something about a partnership. Fett's wounds eventually healed, and for a while, he and Dengar made quite a team.

Six years later, Boba Fett and Dengar tracked the *Millennium Falcon* to Nar Shaddaa. The Hutts still held Han Solo and Leia Organa Solo responsible for the death of Jabba, and both Rebels were wanted alive so the Hutts could watch them die. When Fett and Dengar ambushed the two Rebels, was the first time Solo and Fett had come face-to-face since the battle at the Great Pit of Carkoon. The Rebels escaped to Byss, but they were pursued by Boba Fett and Dengar in Fett's backup ship, *Slave II*. However, only the *Millennium Falcon* had been cleared to enter Byss' planetary security shields, and the closing shields destroyed *Slave II*'s control rudder. As Boba Fett struggled to regain control of the damaged ship, Dengar swore he would never work with him again.

The bounty hunters went their separate ways, and Fett was confident he'd have his chance Solo again. Until then, he was just killing time.

11001010001110110111101101010101010100100011000111010011101000001111001010001110110011000111010
01

111100101010000111011101111011010101010101010100100101010110110100100001010100010101001010010

III: SUBSTANTIAL REWARDS:
BOUNTY HUNTER COLLECTIBLES

Okay. So practically everyone knows about the missile-firing Boba Fett action figure that wasn't. And the non–missile-firing version that was. And a bunch of other, more recent versions of Fett in the 3 3/4-inch figure line. They may even know about the 12-inch Boba Fett collector figures.

But was there *really* any other bounty hunters merchandise that a *Star Wars* collector might be seeking? Scratch your head no more, for as the accompanying list shows, there has been an abundance of bounty hunter collectibles featuring far more than just the baaad dude in the cool costume with the jet pack on his back.

From 4-LOM to Zuckuss—an especially confusing journey given Kenner's earlier mix-up of the two bounty hunters' names—there have been scores of collectibles with the mugs of those mercenaries who have no loyalties other than to themselves. Hated by most of the Rebellion's freedom fighters, scorned but tolerated by the Emperor's minions, the galaxy's bounty hunters have been a minor but integral part of the *Star Wars* galaxy since Boba Fett was first introduced in the infamous "Star Wars Holiday Special" in 1978. The 10-minute-long animated segment in which Fett was introduced as a seeming friend and helper to Luke Skywalker was the most tolerable thing about the entire show and sparked anticipation once it became known that Fett would play a role in *The Empire Strikes Back*.

The story of the missile-firing Boba Fett has been told earlier in this book. But it largely was that bittersweet feeling of thousands of kids—getting a cool-looking figure but without the exciting action feature that they had dreamed of—that spurred the interest in Fett even before *Empire* opened. It's amazing how many people even today insist that the Boba Fett action figure they received in the white mailer box actually did have the missile-firing feature, despite concrete evidence that none were ever sent out. Of course, those who claim to have gotten the real one never seem to have it around anymore because (a) their mother threw it away, (b) the dog bit its head off, or (c) they burned and

1110010100011101101111011010101010101010010001100011000111010011101000001111001010
10110111101101

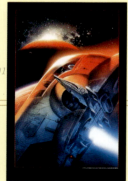

AURRA SING

then buried it in a backyard ritual. The desire to own an authentic vintage Fett missile-firing figure is so strong that one particularly rare prototype exchanged hands in a private sale for what was whispered to be more than $15,000. Lots of carefully crafted bootlegs have also surfaced, so buyer beware!

But you don't have to pay the price of a new car to get a nice Boba Fett collectible, since there is such a variety of vintage and recent items from which to choose. The strong, mostly silent one appears on lots of licensed T-shirts all around the world, caps, socks, Underoos underwear, Halloween costumes, British pajama sets, and even a high-end leather jacket from Japan. He is the central character in a line of bedding from Bibb Co. manufactured in 1980 and a bath towel made by WestPoint Stevens in 1997.

Certainly among the coolest items are two at the very high end. First and foremost is Fett himself, or at least the next best (and safest!) thing in the form of Don Post Studios' $5,000 life-size mannequin that reproduces in fiberglass, cloth, and metal the actual Boba Fett costume from the Lucasfilm Archives. For true Fettishists, it is the one piece for which to scrimp and save a lifetime; the underlying mannequin was cast from the body of Jeremy Bulloch, the genial British actor who played the bounty hunter in *Empire* and *Return of the Jedi*. Don Post also makes "popularly" priced and LFL Archives versions of Fett's helmet alone (Riddell made one at 40 percent scale in 1997). The second high-end item is noted comic-industry sculptor Randy Bowen's bronze Fett sculpture, produced in an edition of fifty in 1997 for $3,000 and now available only on the secondary market. Another piece of artistry is Greg Aronowitz's Boba Fett ceramic busts for Legends in Dimensions, available in two different paint schemes to mark the different coloring jobs on the bounty hunter's costumes in *Empire* and *Jedi*.

In action-figure size, there have been a number of different sculpts or paint schemes for 3 3/4-inch Boba Fett figures and three 12-inch line collector figures. Hasbro and Galoob have a

done him smaller—no more than an inch high—and a bit larger at 6 inches for the Epic Force line of posed figures. Fett is available in several sizes in vinyl from Applause. But one of the favorite items of a true Fettophile is a *sericel*—or limited-manufacture animation cel—from a scene in the "Holiday Special" cartoon where Boba was introduced to the world.

Fett's partners in crime aboard the bridge of the Empire's Star Destroyer in *Empire* haven't fared nearly as well, although there are a surprising number of items depicting most of that horde of hunters—even though most casual fans of the films (as opposed to diehard collectors) don't even know their names, since none are mentioned onscreen.

The lack of recognition led to one very bad case of mistaken identity in Toyland, when Kenner called 4-LOM Zuckuss and vice versa in its line of action figures that followed *Empire*. The error wasn't recognized until many years later, when the writers of West End Games, role-playing game books, pointed out to Lucasfilm that in the *Star Wars* naming convention, droid names nearly always had a letter/number combination while living creatures did not. So after a decade of misuse, 4-LOM (named by a wag at Industrial Light & Magic as shorthand for "For the Love of Money") and Zuckuss changed names. Most fans didn't notice until Kenner issued the new version of the action figures.

4-LOM, like most of the other bounty hunters, also appeared in smaller scale in Galoob playsets at about 1 inch high and even in the form of West End Games pot metal figures. For sheer fun, though, little could match the miniature transforming head playsets from Galoob, barely bigger than a walnut but with a really tiny representation of the bounty hunter inside.

The bounty hunters have been favorites in print, especially in Decipher's *Star Wars* customizable card games and many Topps cards series. Their ships have appeared on cards as small but colorful images, as well.

11001010001110110111101101010101 01101111101101 0110011000111010

0011000111010011101000001111001010001110110111101101010101010101001001010101101101001000010101010010

Besides Boba Fett, another collector favorite has long been IG-88, the gray killer droid that was the subject of an elusive 15-inch figure in the initial Kenner line. The last large figure to be produced, and the only one to be sold in *just* an *Empire* carton, it was also in the shortest supply. That's why the IG-88 "doll" tends to fetch the highest amounts in auctions, sometimes more than $500 if truly mint in a mint box.

But the character besides Fett that fans most love to hate is Greedo. His fame was assured when the cocky and stupid bounty hunter went to the Mos Eisley cantina to collect Han Solo and the hefty reward for his capture. Whoever shot first, Greedo has been immortalized in a Don Post over-the-head mask and separate hands, a Greg Aronowitz bust, large and small figures, and even his portrait on the side of small paper cups. Greedo sprang back into the forefront of fans' consciousness when his famous cantina encounter with Han Solo was recut in the *Star Wars* Special Edition to indicate that Greedo, not Han, had shot first.

A look at the list shows that even little-known hunters such as Bossk, Boushh (Leia's alter ego), the bedraggled Dengar, Zuckuss, and Snoova (Chewbacca's alter ego) have action figures and other merchandise plastered with their likenesses. Even Aurra Sing, seen so briefly in *The Phantom Menace,* can claim a couple of pieces of merchandise—most notably the 12-inch figure that accompanies this book, with undoubtedly more to come.

And although bounty hunters are usually loners by trade, there are many items that show them in groups, including a 23-karat gold card from the Scoreboard in 1994. Best of all, Ralph McQuarrie's haunting *Empire* production illustration of the group of bounty hunters, bathed in an eerie orange tone, has shown up on stickers, postcards, mouse pads, and T-shirts. Pieces like that are not only true to the artist's concept, they *are* the artist's concept.

COSTUMES/MASKS

UNITED STATES

Greedo mask
Don Post Studios, 1997

Greedo hands
Don Post Studios, 1997

GAMES

UNITED STATES

Greedo gaming figurine
West End Games, 1988

Greedo CCG card (black border)
Decipher, 1996

Greedo CCG card (black border)
Decipher, 1998

HOUSEHOLD AND KITCHEN RELATED

UNITED STATES

Greedo Dixie cup
American Can Co., 1980

JEWELRY

UNITED STATES

Greedo vinyl key chain
Applause, 1997

Greedo die-cast key chain
Placo Toys, 1998

PLAQUES, SCULPTURES, AND LIMITED EDITIONS

Greedo bust
Legends in 3 Dimensions, 1998

STAMPS/COINS

Greedo Power of the Force coin
Kenner, 1984

TOYS: ACTION FIGURES, DOLLS, AND RELATED

UNITED STATES

Greedo action figure (SW card)
Kenner, 1979

Greedo action figure (ESB card)
Kenner, 1980

Greedo action figure (ROTJ card)
Kenner, 1983

Greedo action figure (orange card)
Kenner, 1996

Greedo action figure (green card)
Kenner, 1997

Greedo 12" action figure (flap box)
Kenner, 1997

Greedo 12" action figure (window box)
Kenner 1998

Greedo action figure (CommTech card)
Hasbro, 1999

CANADA

Greedo action figure (SW card)
Kenner Canada, 1979

Greedo action figure (ESB card)
Kenner Canada, 1980

Greedo action figure (ROTJ card)
Kenner Canada, 1983

Greedo action figure (Trilogo card)
Kenner Canada, 1983

Greedo action figure (orange card)
Kenner Canada, 1996

Greedo action figure (green card)
Kenner Canada, 1997

Greedo 12" action figure (flap box)
Kenner Canada, 1997

Greedo 12" action figure (window box)
Kenner Canada, 1998

Greedo action figure (CommTech card)
Hasbro Canada, 1999

ENGLAND

Greedo action figure (SW card)
Palitoy, 1979

Greedo action figure (ESB card)
Palitoy, 1980

Greedo action figure (ROTJ card)
Palitoy, 1983

Greedo action figure (Trilogo card)
Palitoy, 1983

1110010100011101101111011010 10101010 110001110 0010100011101100110001110010
10110111101101

Greedo action figure (green card)
Kenner, 1997

Greedo action figure (CommTech card)
Hasbro, 1999

FRANCE

Greedo action figure (ROTJ card)
Meccano, 1983

ITALY

Greedo action figure (green card)
Kenner, 1997

Greedo action figure (CommTech card)
Hasbro, 1999

JAPAN

Greedo action figure (SW card)
Takara, 1978

Greedo action figure (ROTJ card)
Tsukuda, 1983

Greedo action figure (CommTech card)
Hasbro Japan, 1999

TOYS: MICRO MACHINE RELATED

UNITED STATES

Greedo Micro Machine figure (sitting)
Galoob, 1994

Greedo mini transforming head playset
Galoob, 1996

Greedo Action Fleet figure
Galoob, 1996

Greedo Micro Machine figure
Galoob, 1996

TOYS: MISCELLANEOUS

UNITED STATES

Greedo 12" vinyl doll
Applause, 1997

Greedo pvc figurine
Applause, 1997

TRADING CARDS

UNITED STATES

Greedo card #107 (Galaxy 1)
Topps, 1993

Greedo Finest card #64
Topps, 1996

BOOKS AND RELATED

UNITED STATES

Bossk card from SW Missions set #11
Scholastic, 1998

GAMES

UNITED STATES

Bossk gaming miniature
West End Games, 1988

Bossk CCG card
Decipher, 1997

Bossk's Mortar Gun CCG card
Decipher, 1997

Hound's Tooth CCG card
Decipher, 1997

Bossk in Hound's Tooth CCG card
Decipher, 1998

Bossk with Mortar Gun CCG card
Decipher, 1999

TOYS: ACTION FIGURES, DOLLS, AND RELATED

UNITED STATES

Bossk action figure (white mailer box)
Kenner, 1980

Bossk action figure (ESB card)
Kenner, 1980

Bossk action figure (ROTJ card)
Kenner, 1983

Bossk action figure (green card)
Kenner, 1997

CANADA

Bossk action figure (ESB card)
Kenner Canada, 1980

Bossk action figure (ROTJ card)
Kenner Canada, 1983

Bossk action figure (green card)
Kenner Canada, 1997

ENGLAND

Bossk action figure (ESB card)
Palitoy, 1980

Bossk action figure (ROTJ card)
Palitoy, 1983

00110001110100111010000011110010100011101101111011010101010101010100101010110110

Bossk action figure (Trilogo card)
Palitoy, 1984

Bossk action figure (green card)
Kenner, 1997

France

Bossk action figure (ROTJ card)
Meccano, 1983

Italy

Bossk action figure (green card)
Kenner, 1997

Japan

Bossk action figure (ROTJ card)
Tsukuda, 1983

Bossk action figure (green card)
Hasbro Japan, 1997

TOYS: MICRO MACHINE RELATED

United States

Bossk Micro Machine figure
Galoob, 1995

Bossk Action Fleet figure
Galoob, 1996

Hound's Tooth Micro Machine vehicle
Galoob, 1996

Bossk mini transforming head playset
Galoob, 1997

TOYS: MISCELLANEOUS

United States

Bossk pvc figurine
Applause, 1998

TRADING CARDS

United States

Bossk clearzone card E2 (Galaxy 3)
Topps, 1995

Bossk Finest card #36
Topps, 1996

Hound's Tooth card #25 (Vehicles)
Topps, 1997

Bossk tin trading card
Metallic Impressions, 1998

BOOKS AND RELATED

United States

Dengar card from SW Missions set #5
Scholastic, 1998

GAMES

United States

Dengar gaming miniature
West End Games, 1988

Dengar CCG card
Decipher, 1997

Dengar's Blaster Carbine CCG card
Decipher, 1997

Punishing One CCG card
Decipher, 1997

Dengar's Modified Riot Gun CCG card
Decipher, 1998

Dengar with Blaster Carbine CCG card
Decipher, 1999

Dengar in Punishing One CCG card
Decipher, 1999

TOYS: ACTION FIGURES, DOLLS, AND RELATED

United States

Dengar action figure (ESB card)
Kenner, 1981

Dengar action figure (ROTJ card)
Kenner, 1983

Dengar action figure (green card)
Kenner, 1997

Canada

Dengar action figure (ESB card)
Kenner Canada, 1981

Dengar action figure (ROTJ card)
Kenner Canada, 1983

Dengar action figure (green card)
Kenner Canada, 1997

England

Dengar action figure (ESB card)
Palitoy, 1981

Dengar action figure (ROTJ card)
Palitoy, 1983

Dengar action figure (Trilogo card)
Palitoy, 1984

Dengar action figure (green card)
Kenner, 1997

FRANCE

Dengar action figure (ROTJ card)
Meccano, 1983

ITALY

Dengar action figure (green card)
Kenner, 1997

JAPAN

Dengar action figure (ROTJ card)
Tsukuda, 1983

Dengar action figure (green card)
Hasbro Japan, 1997

TOYS: MICRO MACHINE RELATED

UNITED STATES

Dengar Micro Machine figure
Galoob, 1996

TRADING CARDS

UNITED STATES

Dengar clearzone card E6 (Galaxy 3)
Topps, 1995

Dengar Finest card #35
Topps, 1996

Dengar tin trading card
Metallic Impressions, 1998

FILM, VIDEO, AND SLIDES

UNITED STATES

Zuckuss freeze frame slide
Kenner, 1998

GAMES

UNITED STATES

Zuckuss gaming miniature
West End Games, 1988

Zuckuss CCG card
Decipher, 1997

Zuckuss' Snare Rifle CCG card
Decipher, 1997

Mist Hunter CCG card
Decipher, 1997

Zuckuss in Mist Hunter CCG card
Decipher, 1999

STAMPS/COINS

UNITED STATES

Zuckuss Power of the Force coin
Kenner, 1984

TOYS: ACTION FIGURES, DOLLS, AND RELATED

UNITED STATES

Zuckuss action figure (ESB card)
Kenner, 1982

Zuckuss action figure (ROTJ card)
Kenner, 1983

Zuckuss action figure (freeze frame card)
Kenner, 1998

CANADA

Zuckuss action figure (ESB card)
Kenner Canada, 1982

Zuckuss action figure (ROTJ card)
Kenner Canada, 1983

Zuckuss action figure (freeze frame card)
Kenner Canada, 1998

0011000111010011101000001111000110111011011101011110110110101010100100101010101101101001

ENGLAND

Zuckuss action figure (ESB card)
Palitoy, 1982

Zuckuss action figure (ROTJ card)
Palitoy, 1983

Zuckuss action figure (Trilogo card)
Palitoy, 1984

Zuckuss action figure (freeze frame card)
Kenner, 1998

FRANCE

Zuckuss action figure (ROTJ card)
Meccano, 1983

ITALY

Zuckuss action figure (freeze frame card)
Kenner, 1998

JAPAN

Zuckuss action figure (ROTJ card)
Tsukuda, 1983

Zuckuss action figure (freeze frame card)
Hasbro Japan, 1998

TOYS: MICRO MACHINE RELATED

UNITED STATES

Zuckuss Micro Machine figure
Galoob, 1996

TRADING CARDS

UNITED STATES

Zuckuss clearzone card E5 (Galaxy 3)
Topps, 1995

Zuckuss Finest card #49
Topps, 1996

GAMES

UNITED STATES

4-LOM gaming miniature
West End Games, 1988

4-LOM CCG card
Decipher, 1997

4-LOM's Concussion Rifle CCG card
Decipher, 1997

4-LOM with Concussion Rifle CCG card
Decipher, 1999

TOYS: ACTION FIGURES, DOLLS, AND RELATED

UNITED STATES

4-LOM action figure (white mailer box)
Kenner, 1983

4-LOM action figure (ESB card)
Kenner, 1983

4-LOM action figure (ROTJ card)
Kenner, 1983

4-LOM action figure (green card)
Kenner, 1997

CANADA

4-LOM action figure (ESB card)
Kenner Canada, 1983

4-LOM action figure (ROTJ card)
Kenner Canada, 1983

4-LOM action figure (green card)
Kenner Canada, 1998

ENGLAND

4-LOM action figure (ESB card)
Palitoy, 1983

4-LOM action figure (ROTJ card)
Palitoy, 1983

4-LOM action figure (Trilogo card)
Palitoy, 1984

4-LOM action figure (green card)
Kenner, 1998

FRANCE

4-LOM action figure (ROTJ card)
Meccano, 1983

AURRA SING

ITALY

4-LOM action figure (green card)
Kenner, 1998

JAPAN

4-LOM action figure (ROTJ card)
Tsukuda, 1983

4-LOM action figure (green card)
Hasbro Japan, 1998

TOYS: MICRO MACHINE RELATED

UNITED STATES

4-LOM Micro Machine figure
Galoob, 1996

4-LOM Action Fleet figure
Galoob, 1996

4-LOM mini transforming head playset
Galoob, 1997

TRADING CARDS

UNITED STATES

4-LOM clearzone card E3 (Galaxy 3)
Topps, 1995

4-LOM Finest card #86
Topps, 1996

BOOKS AND RELATED

UNITED STATES

IG-88 card from SW Missions set #11
Scholastic, 1998

IG-2000 card from SW Missions set #11
Scholastic, 1998

CRAFTS

UNITED STATES

IG-88 sun catcher
Lee Wards, 1980

GAMES

UNITED STATES

IG-88 gaming miniature
West End Games, 1988

IG-2000 CCG card
Decipher, 1997

IG-88 CCG card
Decipher, 1997

IG-88's Neural Inhibitor CCG card
Decipher, 1997

IG-88's Pulse Cannon CCG card
Decipher, 1997

IG-88 in IG-2000 CCG card
Decipher, 1999

IG-88 with Riot Gun CCG card
Decipher, 1999

TOYS: ACTION FIGURES, DOLLS, AND RELATED

UNITED STATES

IG-88 action figure (ESB card)
Kenner, 1980

IG-88 large-size action figure
Kenner, 1980

IG-88 action figure (ROTJ card)
Kenner, 1983

IG-88 action figure
Kenner, 1996

CANADA

IG-88 action figure (ESB card)
Kenner Canada, 1980

IG-88 action figure (ROTJ card)
Kenner Canada, 1983

ENGLAND

IG-88 action figure (ESB card)
Palitoy, 1980

IG-88 action figure (ROTJ card)
Palitoy, 1983

IG-88 action figure (Trilogo card)
Palitoy, 1984

FRANCE

IG-88 action figure (ROTJ card)
Meccano, 1983

JAPAN

IG-88 action figure (ROTJ card)
Tsukuda, 1983

TOYS: MICRO MACHINE RELATED

UNITED STATES

IG-88 Micro Machine figure
Galoob, 1995

IG-88 Action Fleet figure
Galoob, 1995

IG-2000 Micro Machine vehicle
Galoob, 1996

TRADING CARDS

UNITED STATES

IG-88 card #25 (Galaxy 1)
Topps, 1993

IG-88 card #206 (Galaxy 2)
Topps, 1994

IG-88 clearzone card E4 (Galaxy 3)
Topps, 1995

IG-88 Finest card #89
Topps, 1996

IG-2000 card #24 (Vehicles)
Topps, 1997

IG-88 tin trading card
Metallic Impressions, 1998

CERAMICS

UNITED STATES

Princess Leia as Boushh figurine
Sigma, 1983

GAMES

UNITED STATES

Boushh gaming miniature
West End Games, 1988

Boushh CCG card
Decipher, 1999

TOYS: ACTION FIGURES, DOLLS, AND RELATED

UNITED STATES

Princess Leia Organa (Boushh disguise) action figure
(ROTJ card)
Kenner, 1983

Leia in Boushh disguise action figure (SOTE card)
Kenner, 1996

Leia in Boushh disguise action figure (green card)
Kenner, 1997

Leia in Boushh disguise 12" doll
Kenner, 1998

CANADA

Princess Leia Organa (Boushh disguise) action figure
(ROTJ card)
Kenner Canada, 1983

Leia in Boushh disguise action figure (SOTE card)
Kenner Canada, 1996

Leia in Boushh disguise action figure (green card)
Kenner Canada, 1997

ENGLAND

Princess Leia Organa (Boushh disguise) action figure
(ROTJ card)
Palitoy, 1983

Princess Leia Organa (Boushh disguise) action figure
(Trilogo card)
Palitoy, 1984

Leia in Boushh disguise action figure (SOTE card)
Kenner, 1996

Leia in Boushh disguise action figure (green card)
Kenner, 1997

1110010100011101101111011101010101010100100011000111010 0101000111011001100011010
1011011110101

France

Princess Leia Organa (Boushh disguise) action figure
(ROTJ card)
Meccano, 1983

Italy

Leia in Boushh disguise action figure (SOTE card)
Kenner, 1996

Leia in Boushh disguise action figure (green card)
Kenner, 1997

Japan

Princess Leia Organa (Boushh disguise) action figure
(ROTJ card)
Tsukuda, 1983

Leia in Boushh disguise action figure (SOTE card)
Kenner, 1996

Leia in Boushh disguise action figure (green card)
Kenner, 1997

Mexico

Princess Leia Organa (Boushh disguise) action figure
(ROTJ card)
Lily Ledy, 1983

TOYS: MICRO MACHINE RELATED

United States

Boushh Micro Machine figure
Galoob, 1995

Boushh Action Fleet figure
Galoob, 1996

Boushh mini transforming head playset
Galoob, 1996

TOYS: ACTION FIGURE RELATED

United States

Chewbacca in Bounty Hunter Disguise action figure
(SOTE card)
Kenner, 1996

Canada

Chewbacca in Bounty Hunter Disguise action figure
(SOTE card)
Kenner Canada, 1996

England

Chewbacca in Bounty Hunter Disguise action figure
(SOTE card)
Kenner, 1996

Italy

Chewbacca in Bounty Hunter Disguise action figure
(SOTE card)
Kenner, 1996

Japan

Chewbacca in Bounty Hunter Disguise action figure
(SOTE card)
Hasbro Japan, 1996

TOYS: MICRO MACHINE RELATED

United States

Snoova Micro Machine figure
Galoob, 1996

ANIMATION ART

UNITED STATES

Boba Fett: Bounty Hunter sericel
(from "The Star Wars Holiday Special")
Royal Animated Art, 1996

APPAREL

UNITED STATES

Boba Fett pajamas
Charleston Hosiery Mills, 1980

Boba Fett socks
Charleston Hosiery Mills, 1980

Boba Fett boy's Underoos
Union Underwear, 1980

Boba Fett glitter T-shirt
Factors, 1980

Boba Fett by Joe Smith sweatshirt
American Marketing, 1994

Boba Fett embroidered denim jacket
SW Insider, 1995

Boba Fett by Joe Smith T-shirt
American Marketing, 1995

Boba Fett stipple T-shirt
Changes, 1995

Boba Fett (flying) T-shirt
Changes, 1996

Boba Fett for hire T-shirt
Changes, 1997

Boba Fett cap
Fresh Caps, 1997

Boba Fett character cap
Fresh Caps, 1997

Boba Fett Force shirt (head shot)
Frieze, 1997

Boba Fett tie-dye T-shirt
Liquid Blue, 1997

Boba Fett Bounty Wear T-shirt
Changes, 1997

Boba Fett cap
Ralph Marlin, 1997

Boba Fett w/ fireball T-shirt
Changes, 1997

Boba Fett T-shirt (Slave I on back)
Changes, 1998

Boba Fett T-shirt (gun on back)
Changes, 1998

Slave I T-shirt
Liquid Blue, 1998

ENGLAND

Boba Fett pajamas
Wilker Bros., 1980

Boba Fett pajamas
Wilker Bros., 1997

JAPAN

Boba Fett leather jacket
Sunlike Co., 1998

BED AND BATH

UNITED STATES

Boba Fett–style bed sheet set (various bed sizes)
Bibb Co., 1980

Boba Fett–style bedspread (various bed sizes)
Bibb Co., 1980

Boba Fett–style quilt (various bed sizes)
Bibb Co., 1980

Boba Fett–style blanket (various bed sizes)
Bibb Co., 1980

Boba Fett–style curtains (various sizes)
Bibb Co., 1980

Boba Fett/Darth Vader reversible pillowcase
Bibb Co., 1980

Boba Fett–style sleeping bag
Bibb Co., 1980

Boba Fett bath towel
WestPoint Stevens, 1997

BOOKS AND RELATED

UNITED STATES

Boba Fett bookmark
Random House, 1983

Boba Fett "shapemark" bookmark
Antioch, 1996

Boba Fett wallet card
Antioch, 1997

Boba Fett card from SW Missions set #8
Scholastic, 1998

AURRA SING

BUTTONS/BADGES

UNITED STATES

3" Boba Fett button
Factors, 1980

CERAMICS

UNITED STATES

Boba Fett ceramic figurine
Sigma, 1983

Boba Fett ceramic figural mug
Applause, 1995

Slave I collector plate
Hamilton, 1996

Skull insignia medallion/mug
Rawcliffe, 1996

Boba Fett w/ gun medallion/mug
Rawcliffe, 1997

Boba Fett medallion/mug
Rawcliffe, 1997

Boba Fett stein
Metallic Images, 1997

Boba Fett ceramic mug
Applause, 1998

Boba Fett collector plate
Hamilton, 1998

ENGLAND

Boba Fett collector's mug
Downpace Ltd., 1996

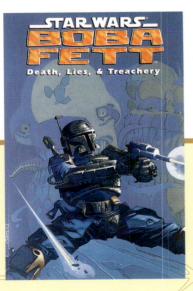

COMIC BOOKS

Boba Fett: Bounty on Bar-Kooda (newsstand and direct
market versions)
Dark Horse, 1995

Boba Fett #2: When the Fat Lady Swings (newsstand and
direct market versions)
Dark Horse, 1996

Boba Fett #3: Murder Most Foul (newsstand and direct
market versions)
Dark Horse, 1997

Boba Fett: Twin Engines of Destruction
Dark Horse, 1997

Boba Fett Wizard 1/2 edition
Dark Horse, 1997

Boba Fett Wizard 1/2 edition (foil stamped)
Dark Horse, 1997

Boba Fett: Death, Lies & Treachery comic compilation
Dark Horse, 1998

Boba Fett: Enemy of the Empire #1
Dark Horse, 1999

Boba Fett: Enemy of the Empire #2
Dark Horse, 1999

Boba Fett: Enemy of the Empire #3
Dark Horse, 1999

Boba Fett: Enemy of the Empire #4
Dark Horse, 1999

COSTUMES

UNITED STATES

SW Boba Fett costume, blue box
Ben Cooper, 1979

Boba Fett child's face mask
Ben Cooper, 1979

ESB Boba Fett costume
Ben Cooper, 1980

ROTJ Boba Fett costume
Ben Cooper, 1983

Boba Fett helmet
Don Post, 1995

Boba Fett deluxe helmet
Don Post, 1997

Boba Fett miniature helmet
Riddell, 1997

MEXICO

Boba Fett paper mask
Papeles Troquelados, 1980

0011000111010011101000001111001010001110110111101101010101010100100101010110110100

CRAFTS

UNITED STATES

Boba Fett figurine paint set
Craft Master, 1980

Boba Fett paint by number
Craft Master, 1980

Boba Fett iron-on (with planet)
Factors, 1980

Bounty Hunters iron-on
Factors, 1980

CUPS/GLASSES

UNITED STATES

Boba Fett plastic collector cup
Coca-Cola, 1979

FILM, VIDEO, AND SLIDES

UNITED STATES

70mm Boba Fett collectible film frame
Willitts, 1996

Boba Fett freeze frame slide
Kenner, 1998

FOOD RELATED

UNITED STATES

Boba Fett Coke Cup
Coca-Cola, 1979

Boba Fett candy head
Topps, 1980

Boba Fett photo cut-out card on Reese's package
Hershey, 1980

Balancing Boba Fett Taco Bell kids meal toy
Applause, 1997

Boba Fett 3-D motion card (found in bags of Doritos/Cheetos)
Frito Lay, 1997

Boba Fett 3-D motion disk (found in bags of Doritos)
Frito Lay, 1997

Boba Fett PEZ (bagged)
PEZ, 1998

Boba Fett PEZ (carded)
PEZ, 1998

ENGLAND

Boba Fett ice-cream wrapper
Lyons Maid, 1980

MEXICO

Boba Fett figurine
Gamesa, 1997

SPAIN

Boba Fett figurine
Sonrics, 1997

Boba Fett ice cream stick
Frigo, 1997

AUSTRALIA

Boba Fett figure cut-out on ice treats box
Streets, 1980

HONG KONG

Boba Fett Sprite bookmark
Coca-Cola, 1980

Boba Fett Sprite ruler
Coca-Cola, 1980

GAMES

Boba Fett gaming miniature
West End Games, 1988

Boba Fett chess piece (bishop)
Danbury Mint, 1993

Boba Fett (Cloud City) CCG card
Decipher, 1997

Slave I CCG card
Decipher, 1997

Boba Fett's Blaster Rifle CCG card
Decipher, 1997

Boba Fett (Special Edition) CCG card (white border)
Decipher, 1997

Boba Fett (Special Edition) CCG card (black border)
Decipher, 1998

Boba Fett with Blaster Rifle CCG card
Decipher, 1998

Boba Fett SW: CCG tournament box
Decipher, 1998

Any Methods Necessary CCG card
Decipher, 1999

Boba Fett in Slave I CCG card
Decipher, 1999

Jodo Kast CCG card
Decipher, 1999

1110010100011101101110   00111010011101000001111001010001110110011000111010
10110111101101

HOUSEHOLD AND KITCHEN RELATED

UNITED STATES

Boba Fett cake pan
Wilton, 1981

Boba Fett Dixie cup
American Can Co., 1981

Boba Fett's ship Slave I Dixie cup
American Can Co., 1981

Boba Fett ornament
Hallmark, 1998

JEWELRY

UNITED STATES

Boba Fett medal
Wallace Berrie, 1980

Boba Fett pin
Hollywood Pins, 1996

Boba Fett pin, "He's No Good to Me Dead"
Hollywood Pins, 1996

Slave I pin
Hollywood Pins, 1996

Boba Fett round insignia pin
Hollywood Pins, 1997

Boba Fett skull insignia pin
Hollywood Pins, 1997

Boba Fett vinyl key chain
Applause, 1997

Boba Fett die-cast key chain
Placo Toys, 1997

Boba Fett w/ gun key chain
Rawcliffe, 1997

Boba Fett skull insignia key chain
Rawcliffe, 1997

CANADA

Boba Fett die-cast key chain
Placo Toys, 1997

JAPAN

Boba Fett ring
J.A.P., 1997

Boba Fett ring (painted)
J.A.P., 1997

LUGGAGE AND CARRYALLS

UNITED STATES

Boba Fett backpack (rectangular)
Pyramid, 1997

Boba Fett backpack (rounded top)
Pyramid, 1997

Boba Fett duffel bag
Pyramid, 1997

Boba Fett luggage with extending handle
Pyramid, 1997

MAGNETS

UNITED STATES

Boba Fett magnet
ATA Boy, 1997

Boba Fett in Cloud City magnet
ATA Boy, 1997

Magic of Myth magnet
Ata Boy, 1998

MAQUETTES

UNITED STATES

Boba Fett torso
Illusive Originals, 1996

0011000111010011101000001111001010001110110111101101010101010100100101010110110100

MODELS

UNITED STATES

Slave I model kit (ESB box)
MPC, 1982

Boba Fett 1/6-scale-vinyl model kit
Screamin', 1994

Boba Fett 1/4 scale-vinyl model kit
Screamin', 1996

Slave I model kit (new art box)
AMT/Ertl, 1997

ENGLAND

Slave I model kit (ESB box)
Airfix, 1982

JAPAN

Slave I vs. The Millennium Falcon metal kit
Tsukuda, 1980

Boba Fett 1/6 scale resin model kit
Kaiyodo, 1993

Boba Fett 1/6 scale vinyl model kit
Kaiyodo, 1993

PEWTER

UNITED STATES

Boba Fett pewter figurine
Rawcliffe, 1994

Slave I pewter ship
Rawcliffe, 1996

PLAQUES, SCULPTURES, AND LIMITED EDITIONS

UNITED STATES

Boba Fett bust (ESB paint scheme)
Legends in 3 Dimension, 1997

Boba Fett bust (ROTJ paint scheme)
Legends in 3 Dimension, 1997

Boba Fett bronze sculpture
Bowen Designs, 1997

Boba Fett life-size mannequin
Don Post, 1998

POSTERS

UNITED STATES

Set of 11 lithographs of Boba Fett costume sketches
by Joe Johnston
Lucasfilm, 1980

Boba Fett poster, 20" x 28"
Factors, 1980

Bounty Hunters by Ralph McQuarrie, 17" x 22"
Topps, 1993

Boba Fett ESB 15th ann. gold mylar poster
Kilian Ent., 1995

Boba Fett: Bounty Hunter by Dave Dorman
Rolling Thunder Graphics, 1995

Slave I poster by Tsuneo Sando
Star Wars Fan Club, 1997

Boba Fett: Fall of a Bounty Hunter by Dave Dorman
Rolling Thunder Graphics, 1998

STAMPS/COINS

UNITED STATES

Boba Fett coin (silver tone)
Kenner, 1984

Boba Fett coin (gold tone)
Kenner, 1984

STANDEES

UNITED STATES

Boba Fett standee
Factors, 1980

Boba Fett standee
Advanced Graphics, 1996

STATIONERY/SCHOOL SUPPLIES

UNITED STATES

Boba Fett birthday card
Drawing Board, 1980

Boba Fett memo pad
Stuart Hall, 1980

Boba Fett notebook
Stuart Hall, 1980

Boba Fett notepad
Stuart Hall, 1980

Boba Fett portfolio
Stuart Hall, 1980

Boba Fett 4" x 6" postcard
Classico, 1994

ENGLAND

Boba Fett die-cut eraser
H.C. Ford, 1980

Boba Fett 5" x 5" framed art
Icarus, 1980

JAPAN

Boba Fett mini head pen
Showanote, 1997

Boba Fett mini head pencil
Showanote, 1997

Boba Fett mini head on a suction cup
Showanote, 1997

STORE DISPLAYS

UNITED STATES

Action figure bin card: Get a Free Boba Fett
Kenner, 1979

Action figure ling display card: Collect all 21, Boba Fett offer
Kenner, 1979

Action figure bin card: Collect all 21, Boba Fett offer with
sticker covering firing backpack
Kenner, 1979

Boba Fett action figure long display card
Kenner, 1979

TINWARE

UNITED STATES

Boba Fett micro tin
Metal Box Co., 1980

TOYS

UNITED STATES

Boba Fett action figure (white mailer box)
Kenner, 1979

Boba Fett action figure (SW card)
Kenner, 1979

Boba Fett large-size action figure (SW box)
Kenner, 1979

Boba Fett action figure (ESB card)
Kenner, 1980

Boba Fett large-size action figure (ESB box)
Kenner, 1980

Slave I vehicle
Kenner, 1980

Slave I vehicle with back drop
Kenner, 1980

Boba Fett action figure (ROTJ card—photo w/ flame-thrower)
Kenner, 1983

Boba Fett action figure (ROTJ card—photo on Skiff)
Kenner, 1983

Boba Fett action figure (Droids card)
Kenner, 1984

Boba Fett action figure (orange card)
Kenner, 1995

Boba Fett action figure (ESB paint scheme)
Kenner, 1996

Deluxe Boba Fett action figure
Kenner, 1996

Boba Fett action figure (green card)
Kenner, 1996

Boba Fett's Slave I vehicle (SOTE box)
Kenner, 1996

Boba Fett 12" action figure
Kenner, 1996

Boba Fett's Slave I vehicle (green box)
Kenner, 1997

Boba Fett action figure (freeze frame card)
Kenner, 1998

Electronic Boba Fett 12" action figure
Kenner, 1998

0011000111010011101000001111001010001110110111101101010101010100100101010110110100

Boba Fett action figure (SW card)
Kenner Canada, 1979

Boba Fett action figure (ESB card)
Kenner Canada, 1980

Boba Fett action figure (ROTJ card)
Kenner Canada, 1983

Boba Fett action figure (Droids card)
Kenner Canada, 1984

Boba Fett action figure (orange card)
Kenner Canada, 1995

Deluxe Boba Fett action figure
Kenner Canada, 1996

Boba Fett action figure (green card)
Kenner Canada, 1996

Boba Fett action figure (freeze frame card)
Kenner Canada, 1998

ENGLAND

Boba Fett action figure (ESB card)
Palitoy, 1980

Slave I vehicle
Palitoy, 1980

Boba Fett action figure (ROTJ card)
Palitoy, 1983

Boba Fett action figure (Trilogo card)
Kenner, 1984

Boba Fett action figure (orange card)
Kenner, 1995

Deluxe Boba Fett action figure
Kenner, 1996

Boba Fett action figure (green card)
Kenner, 1996

Boba Fett action figure (freeze frame card)
Kenner, 1998

ITALY

Boba Fett action figure (orange card)
Kenner, 1995

Deluxe Boba Fett action figure
Kenner, 1996

Boba Fett action figure (green card)
Kenner, 1996

Boba Fett action figure (freeze frame card)
Kenner, 1998

JAPAN

Boba Fett action figure (ROTJ card)
Tsukuda, 1983

Boba Fett action figure (orange card)
Hasbro Japan, 1995

Deluxe Boba Fett action figure
Hasbro Japan, 1996

Boba Fett action figure (green card)
Hasbro Japan, 1996

Boba Fett action figure (freeze frame card)
Hasbro Japan, 1998

TOYS: ELECTRONIC

UNITED STATES

Boba Fett electronic key chain
Tiger, 1997

Boba Fett room alarm
Tiger, 1998

TOYS: MICRO MACHINE RELATED

UNITED STATES

Slave I Micro Machine vehicle
Galoob, 1994

Slave I Micro Machine vehicle (silver)
Galoob, 1995

Boba Fett Micro Machine figure
Galoob, 1995

Slave I X-ray Fleet vehicle
Galoob, 1995

Boba Fett/Cloud City transforming playset (black box)
Galoob, 1996

Boba Fett/Cloud City transforming playset (striped box)
Galoob, 1996

Boba Fett mini transforming head playset
Galoob, 1996

Slave I Action Fleet vehicle
Galoob, 1996

Slave I vehicle (X-ray fleet–sized but painted)
Galoob, 1996

Slave I die-cast vehicle
Galoob, 1997

Slave I Micro-micro Machine vehicle (from limited 3-ship set)
Galoob, 1997

Slave I transforming playset
Galoob, 1998

CANADA

Slave I Action Fleet vehicle
Galoob, 1996

Boba Fett/Cloud City transforming playset
Galoob, 1996

GERMANY

Micro Machine Slave I and Boba Fett (carded)
Ideal, 1997

JAPAN

Slave I Action Fleet vehicle
Tsukuda, 1996

Micro Machine Slave I and Boba Fett (carded)
Tsukuda, 1997

TOYS: MISCELLANEOUS

UNITED STATES

Die-cast Slave I
Kenner, 1980

Boba Fett Micro Collection die-cast figurine
Kenner, 1982

Boba Fett Action Master
Kenner, 1995

Boba Fett 12" vinyl figure
Applause, 1995

Boba Fett pvc figurine
Applause, 1996

Boba Fett Bend Em
Just Toys, 1996

Slave I figure maker
Kenner, 1997

Boba Fett Epic Force figure
Kenner, 1997

Boba Fett's Armor
Kenner, 1998

CANADA

Boba Fett Epic Force figure
Kenner Canada, 1997

JAPAN

Wind-up Boba Fett tin toy
Osaka Tin Toy Institute, 1998

TRADING CARDS

UNITED STATES

Boba Fett Galaxy 1 cards #13, 127
Topps, 1993

Boba Fett Galaxy 2 cards #211, 269, foil card 10, promo P6
Topps, 1994

Boba Fett Galaxy 3 cards #301, 347, 358, clearzone E1,
promo P1
Topps, 1995

Boba Fett Dark Horse card DH2
Topps, 1995

Boba Fett tin card (from ESB boxed tin card set)
Metallic Images, 1995

Boba Fett Shadows of the Empire cards #82, 88, promo
SOTE 5
Topps, 1996

Slave I Vehicles cards #23, 69, 97, C2
Topps, 1997

Boba Fett 24k gold card (ESB series)
Authentic Images, 1997

Boba Fett 24k gold card (ROTJ series)
Authentic Images, 1997

WATCHES AND CLOCKS

UNITED STATES

Boba Fett 3D hologram watch
3D Arts, 1990

Boba Fett flip-open watch with Death Star case
Hope Ind., 1997

Boba Fett flip-open watch
Hope Ind., 1997

Boba Fett limited edition watch (silver)
Fossil, 1998

Boba Fett limited edition watch (gold)
Fossil, 1998

CANADA

Boba Fett LCD watch
Watchit, 1997

AUSTRALIA

Boba Fett flip top watch (space battle card)
Playworks, 1997

Boba Fett flip top watch (C-3PO card)
Playworks, 1997

BUTTONS/BADGES

UNITED STATES

Aurra Sing collector badge
SW Fan Club, 2000

COMIC BOOKS

UNITED STATES

Star Wars Bounty Hunters #1
Dark Horse, 1999

GAMES

UNITED STATES

Aurra Sing Young Jedi game card
Decipher, 1999

Aurra Sing's Blaster Rifle Young Jedi game card
Decipher, 1999

TOYS: ACTION FIGURE RELATED

UNITED STATES

Aurra Sing 12" action figure
Hasbro, 2000

Aurra Sing action figure (carded)
Hasbro, 2001

COLLECTIBLES WITH MULTIPLE BOUNTY HUNTERS

APPAREL

UNITED STATES

Bounty Hunters by Ralph McQuarrie T-shirt
Ralph American Marketing, 1995

Bounty Hunters by Ralph McQuarrie necktie
Ralph Marlin, 1997

Bounty Hunters action figureT-shirt
Changes, 1997

BOOKS AND RELATED

UNITED STATES

Tales of the Bounty Hunters
Bantam, 1996

Battle of the Bounty Hunters Pop-Up Book
Dark Horse, 1996

Bounty Hunters Mission set #11
Scholastic, 1998

The Bounty Hunter Wars Book 1: The Mandalorian Armor
Bantam, 1998

The Bounty Hunter Wars Book 2: Slave Ship
Bantam, 1998

The Bounty Hunter Wars Book 3: Hard Merchandise
Bantam, 1999

ENGLAND

Jabba the Hutt and Bounty Hunters Microfax
Henderson Publishing, 1997

COMIC BOOKS

UNITED STATES

Kenner Shadows of the Empire (Boba Fett/IG-88 cover)
Dark Horse, 1996

COMPUTER RELATED

UNITED STATES

Bounty Hunters by Ralph McQuarrie mouse pad
Moustrak, 1995

GAMES

UNITED STATES

Tatooine Manhunt gaming scenario
West End Games, 1988

Bounty Hunters gaming miniatures boxed set
West End Games, 1988

Galaxy Guide 10: Bounty Hunters
West End Games, 1993

Bounty Hunters #1 gaming miniatures blister pack
West End Games, 1994

Bounty Hunters #2 gaming miniatures blister pack
West End Games, 1994

Bounty Hunters #3 gaming miniatures blister pack
West End Games, 1994

No Disintegrations! Adventures for bounty hunters
West End Games, 1997

HOUSEHOLD AND KITCHEN RELATED

UNITED STATES

Bounty Hunters Dixie cup
American Can Co., 1983

ENGLAND

Bounty Hunters place mat
Icarus Co., 1980

MAGNETS

UNITED STATES

Bounty Hunters magnet
ATA Boy, 1997

PLAQUES, SCULPTURES, AND LIMITED EDITIONS

UNITED STATES

Bounty Hunter statues (Boba Fett, Bossk, and Zuckuss)
Applause, 1996

STATIONERY/SCHOOL SUPPLIES

UNITED STATES

Bounty Hunters McQuarrie art sticker
OSWFC, 1980

TOYS: ACTION FIGURE RELATED

UNITED STATES

Boba Fett vs. IG-88
Kenner, 1996

CANADA

Boba Fett vs. IG-88
Kenner Canada, 1996

ENGLAND

Boba Fett vs. IG-88
Kenner, 1996

ITALY

Boba Fett vs. IG-88
Kenner, 1996

TOYS: MICRO MACHINE RELATED

UNITED STATES

Micro Machine Bounty Hunters figure set
Galoob, 1998

TRADING CARDS

UNITED STATES

Bounty Hunters 23k gold card
Scoreboard, 1994

Bounty Hunters tin card set
Metallic Impressions, 1998

WALL DECORATIONS

UNITED STATES

Bounty Hunters by Ralph McQuarrie Chromart
Zanart, 1995

001100011101001110100000011110010100011101101011101101010101010100100101010110110100

BIBLIOGRAPHY

I.   HUNTERS IN THE MAKING

    Arnold, Alan. *Once Upon a Galaxy: A Journal of the Making of The Empire Strikes Back.*
        London: Sphere Books, 1980.

    Attias, Diana and Lindsay Smith. *Star Wars: The Empire Strikes Back Notebook.*
        New York: Ballantine Books, 1980.

    Bouzereau, Laurent. *Star Wars: The Annotated Screenplays.* New York: Del Rey, 1997.

    Daley, Brian. *Star Wars: The Empire Strikes Back: The National Public Radio Dramatization.*
        New York: Ballantine Books, 1995.

    Goodwin, Archie and Al Williamson. *Star Wars* (collected comic strips, limited edition).
        West Plains, Missouri: Russ Cochran, 1991.

    Johnston, Joe and Nilo Rodis-Jamero. *Star Wars: The Empire Strikes Back Sketchbook.*
        New York: Ballantine Books, 1980.

    Peecher, John Phillip, editor. *The Making of Star Wars: Return of the Jedi.*
        New York: Del Rey, 1983.

    Sansweet, Steve with Josh Ling. *Star Wars: The Action Figure Archive.* San Francisco: Chronicle Books, 1999.

    Star Wars Galaxy Collector magazine.

    Star Wars Galaxy magazine.

    Star Wars Insider magazine.

    Star Wars magazine (UK).

    Vaz, Mark Cotta. *The Secrets of Star Wars: Shadows of the Empire.* New York: Del Rey, 1996.

II. THE SAGA OF THE BOUNTY HUNTERS

    Anderson, Kevin J., editor. *Star Wars: Tales From Jabba's Palace.* New York: Bantam Books, 1996.

    ____. *Star Wars: Tales of the Bounty Hunters.* New York: Bantam Books, 1996.

    Goodwin, Archie, and Al Williamson. *Classic Star Wars,* nos. 1–20. Milwaukie, Oreg:
        Dark Horse Comics, 1992-94.

    Jeter, K.W. *Star Wars: The Mandalorian Armor.* New York: Bantam Books, 1998.

    ____. *Star Wars: Slave Ship.* New York: Bantam Books, 1998.

    ____. *Star Wars: Hard Merchandise.* New York: Bantam Books, 1999.

    Mangels, Andy. *Star Wars: The Essential Guide to Characters.* New York: Del Rey, 1995.

    ____. *Star Wars: Boba Fett—Twin Engines of Destruction.* Milwaukie, Oreg: Dark Horse Comics, 1997.

    Manning, Russ. *Classic Star Wars: The Early Adventures.* Milwaukie, Oreg: Dark Horse Comics, 1997.

    Perry, Steve. *Shadows of the Empire.* New York: Bantam Books, 1996.

    Schultz, Mark. *Star Wars: The Bounty Hunters—Scoundrel's Wages.* Milwaukie, Oreg: Dark Horse Comics, 1999.

    Star Wars: A New Hope. 20th Century-Fox. 1977.

    Star Wars: The Empire Strikes Back. Lucasfilm Ltd., 1980.

    Star Wars: Return of the Jedi. Lucasfilm Ltd., 1983.

    Stuart, Rick D. *Star Wars Galaxy Guide 10: Bounty Hunters.* Honesdale, Penn: West End Games, 1994.

    Truman, Tim. *Star Wars: Prelude to Rebellion.* Milwaukie, Oreg: Dark Horse Comics, 1998–1999.

    ____. *Star Wars: Outlander.* Milwaukie, Oreg: Dark Horse Comics, 1998–1999.

    ____. *Star Wars: The Bounty Hunters—Aurra Sing* one-shot. Milwaukie, Oreg: Dark Horse Comics, 1999.

    Veitch, Tom. *Star Wars: Dark Empire.* Milwaukie, Oreg: Dark Horse Comics, 1993.

    ____. *Star Wars: Dark Empire II.* Milwaukie, Oreg: Dark Horse Comics, 1995.

    Wagner, John. *Star Wars: Shadows of the Empire,* nos. 1–6. Milwaukie, Oreg: Dark Horse Comics, 1997.

    ____. *Star Wars: Boba Fett: Salvage.* Milwaukie, Oreg: Dark Horse Comics, 1997.

    ____. *Star Wars: Boba Fett: Death, Lies, & Treachery.* Milwaukie, Oreg: Dark Horse Comics, 1998.

    ____. *Star Wars: Boba Fett: Enemy of the Empire,* nos. 1–4. Milwaukie, Oreg: Dark Horse Comics, 1998–1999.

    Windham, Ryder. *Star Wars: Battle of the Bounty Hunters.* Milwaukie, Oreg: Dark Horse Comics, 1996.

    Wolverton, Dave. *The Hunt for Han Solo.* New York: Scholastic, 1998.